Contents

Dobroder

Acknowledgements

In writing this book, I received advice and assistance from many people. Portions of the book were written after long and intensive discussions with many individuals, of the various and complex situations facing the Indian. My colleagues in both the province of Alberta and the National Indian Brotherhood helped, through the process of formal deliberation, to crystallize some of the issues. I hold none of them responsible for what is contained here; the views are my own. But to all who helped formulate my thoughts or gave critical suggestions and ideas, I am most grateful.

The only way I can return their assistance is through this book, if, because of their help, it stimulates new thoughts, different approaches, provokes discussion and, more importantly, initiates action in the areas of their particular concern. Perhaps in a modest way the book may help to create a better life for the next generation of Canadian Indians.

I wish to express my gratitude to Chief Robert Smallboy who, through his wisdom, gave me the opportunity to gain a deeper understanding· of Indianness in the twentieth century. I extend my thanks to Eugene Steinhauer, executive director of the Alberta Native Communications Society; to Edward Bellerose and George Manuel, both Core staff members of the Indian Association of Alberta, and to David Courchene, president of the Manitoba Indian Brotherhood, for the discussions which helped to clarify many of the pressing problems facing us.

I would like to acknowledge the efforts of William Wacko, for providing some of the data and reference material and for his attempts to help find locations where I could write without interference. I extend my thanks to my publisher for his perseverance, patience and encouragement; to Susan Kent for her editorial assistance; to Maxine Thomas for her assistance in typing and to Mrs. Peggy Robbins for her diligence in proofreading patiently the draft writings.

I am particularly grateful for the assistance of Ed Ogle of Calgary, who gave so generously of his time to discuss the manuscript with me.

I offer my special gratitude to the many elder Indians whose views, expressed during the many local meetings I attended, helped to shape my thinking.

And to my wife, my appreciation can never adequately be expressed.

Introduction

Thirty years ago, Indian Nations in Canada stood at an important cross-roads, facing the prospect of termination. The Liberal government of the day proposed doing away with Indian reserves, status and identity. It was, for Indian Nations, literally a question of survival.

Many of my relatives, friends, mentors, teachers and colleagues both in Alberta and elsewhere in Canada who shared in the task of developing our responses to the threat facing our nations have now passed on. To them, particularly for the strength, determination, calm, foresight and dignity they displayed during our time of adversity, we owe a continuing and lasting debt of gratitude. As well, I express my continuing gratitude to those still living.

The Unjust Society was written to capture the issues as we then saw them. It represented an attempt to bring to the Canadian public, perhaps for the first time, a voice that was ours, a voice that reflected First Nation thoughts and reactions to the situation facing us. It described the political environment of the late 1960s and the state of Indian/White relations. It presented the challenges facing First Nation political leaders and their communities and provided a glimpse of the contemporary Indian political movement in its embryonic stages. I neither apologize for nor seek to justify how First Nation peoples reacted to the world as it then was and the world as we then saw it.

As we enter a new millennium, I think it is appropriate to bring *The Unjust Society* back into print as a way of sharing, with those not yet born at the time, a chronicle of our struggle, our thoughts and our experiences. At least in a preliminary fashion, I think it is also an opportunity to take stock of what has transpired since the book's original publication. Much has happened since then, though how much has really changed remains open to question.

One can point to changes in the Canadian Constitution as evidence of the advances that the Canadian and Indian societies have made in their relationship with one another. We now have a Charter of Rights and Freedoms, which didn't exist at the time *The Unjust Society* was first published. In addition, since 1982, we have had constitutional provisions enshrining Aboriginal and Treaty rights—provisions which did not exist in 1969. Together, these constitutional developments appeared at first to offer new opportunities for both Canadians generally and Indian First Nations in Canada to advance, and perhaps restructure, a relationship in desperate need of repair.

Yet despite the 1982 constitutional changes, Canadians collectively experienced armed confrontations during the "Summer of Oka" in 1990, and again at Gustafsen Lake in 1995. Each of these events demonstrated how dangerously close to the edge the state of Indian/White relations in Canada really is. The 1971 murder of Helen Betty Osborne in Manitoba; the fatal shooting of John Joseph Harper by a constable of the Winnipeg Police Department on March 9, 1988; the eleven-year wrongful imprisonment of Donald Marshall in Nova Scotia; the killing of Dudley George at an unarmed occupation of Stoney Point traditional lands near Sarnia, Ontario on September 6, 1995, by an Ontario Provincial Police officer; and the killing of Connie Jacobs and her nine-year-old son Ty on March 24, 1998, by an RCMP officer at the T'suu T'ina Reserve in Alberta serve as vivid reminders that all is not well in Indian country.

While there have been discernable changes in the Canadian political landscape since 1969, so far—regrettably—these remain no more than promises yet to be fulfilled. Unfortunately, at the core, the issues this book identified in the late 1960s are issues still unresolved today.

Since *The Unjust Society* was written, the indifference of Canadian society to our situation, the stereotyping of First Nation peoples and the social conditions First Nations face have been explored in graphic detail by parliamentary reports, including "Indian Self-Government in Canada" (the Penner Report), published in 1983; by the 1991 Manitoba Aboriginal Justice Inquiry and a myriad of other justice inquiries across Canada; by prime ministerial statements, particularly those made at the start of each of the constitutional conferences on Aboriginal matters, which began in 1983 and culminated most recently in the Charlottetown Accord of 1992; and by the voluminous *Report of the Royal Commission on Aboriginal Peoples* released in 1997.

In 1969, the government of Canada indicated clearly that it was not prepared to recognize "Aboriginal rights." This position began to alter significantly after the 1973 Supreme Court of Canada ruling in *Calder v. the Queen*. In that decision, the Supreme Court justices were evenly split on whether or not the existence of Aboriginal title in British Columbia ought to be recognized. At approximately the same time, the James Bay Cree succeeded through litigation in forcing both the government of Quebec and Hydro Quebec to the negotiating table, and there the Cree were successful in having their Aboriginal interests addressed prior to the completion of the James Bay hydroelectric project. These two events gave the Trudeau government an opportunity to revise its position on Aboriginal rights. They created a process through which comprehensive claims could be addressed by governments and First Nation representatives in those areas of Canada where no Treaties had been negotiated. This has resulted in modern-day Treaties in Canada, beginning with the James Bay and Northern Quebec Agreement. Since then, a number of comprehensive claims agreements have been concluded in the Northwest Territories and Yukon.

The government of British Columbia officially joined the Treaty-making process under a cloud of continuing litigation and social unrest. Ostensibly, the B.C. Treaty process was created to provide a forum enabling British Columbia, Canada and First Nations to address Indian claims based on Aboriginal title in the province. Both the Treaty-making process and the approach taken to it have been contested by some First Nations and strongly resisted by some non-Aboriginal interests in the province. Despite both the strong support by the current British Columbia government for a negotiated Treaty process to address the issues surrounding Aboriginal title, and the Supreme Court commentary on the nature of Aboriginal rights in the 1997 *Delgamuukw* decision, it is at this point uncertain whether the process will survive the political opposition being mounted by a variety of non-Aboriginal interest groups and political parties.

The Inuit of Nunavut—the Inuit homeland which was officially recognized on April 1, 1999—appear to be the Aboriginal group who have advanced furthest in securing an agreement that enables them to enjoy and exercise the broadest range of Aboriginal rights. Whether this will be a lasting achievement, or one which becomes the contemporary equivalent of what happened to the Metis people with the creation of the province of Manitoba in 1870, remains to be seen.

Other than the reference to Treaty and Treaty rights in the Canadian Constitution, the policy approach employed by the federal government in addressing the broad issues of Treaty, Treaty relationships and Treaty rights has not advanced much beyond the confines of the 1969 White Paper. Of all the Aboriginal groups, the Treaty Indian leadership appears to have made the least headway and achieved the least success in securing changes to government policy required for addressing the question of Treaty, Treaty relationships and Treaty rights. The most they have succeeded in doing is securing Canada's tentative and uncertain undertaking to "explore" the issues underlying the Treaties. Yet despite the lack of discernible progress in altering government policies regarding Treaties, the abiding commitment and the deep spiritual feelings attached to Treaties remain indelibly embedded in the psyche of First Nation Elders.

In 1969, the government of Canada proposed and adopted an approach whereby Indian Treaties were to be understood only as literally read in documents produced by Crown representatives. Under this method of Treaty interpretation, only those documents entitled "Articles of Treaty" would be considered, and only in the context of the specific or express words they contained. Any other documents, such as Treaty Commissioners' reports or the written reports of other witnesses present at Treaty-making, as well as the Indian understanding of the Treaties at the time of their negotiation, would be excluded as a basis for determining the nature of the Treaty and the rights contained within it.

The approach adopted in 1969 by the federal government has now been rejected by the Supreme Court of Canada. In accordance with various Supreme Court of Canada judgements, the Canadian judiciary is now in part required, when considering matters pertaining to Treaties or Treaty rights, to seek "an Indian understanding of the Treaties" and to remember that "the honour of the Crown" is at stake on these issues. Among other things, the courts now require that Indian Treaty rights be "liberally construed." This means that Treaties and Treaty rights ought to be interpreted or understood, where possible, in broad terms rather than being defined and understood in their narrow and limited technical meanings. This new approach adopted by the courts with respect to

Indian Treaties has gone a long way in providing guidance for contemporary discussions where Treaties and Treaty rights are at issue.

In addition to securing these legal decisions domestically, Canada's First Nations have embarked on a major effort aimed at seeking international recognition for Indian Treaties and Treaty rights. They have succeeded in creating an international profile for Indian Nations and have found international forums through which they have managed to engage the attention of the world community.

Yet outside of litigation or international action, no forum presently exists wherein First Nations may address and resolve the fundamental issues underlying their Treaty relationship with the Crown. Now, as at the time this book was written, the government of Canada continues to deny the existence of substantive Treaty rights across a broad policy spectrum covering matters pertaining to land, resources, health, education, and social and economic matters. The Indian First Nations continue to insist that these matters form an integral part of their relationship with the Crown, but as yet with no tangible results.

In part, this stonewalling is attributable to the unwillingness of Canadian government policy-makers and the Canadian judiciary to recognize the original sovereign ownership of Canada by Indian First Nations. In the United States, the American judiciary has since 1832 recognized Indian Nations as "sovereign nations" from whom the United States derived its sovereign title. From that premise, the American judiciary has been able to recognize Indian Treaties negotiated in the United States as being negotiated between two sovereign powers: Indian Nations on the one hand and the American nation on the other. The U.S. judiciary acknowledges the simple historical fact that, through Treaties, Americans received from the Indian Nations the rights they enjoy, while the Indian Nations continue through Treaty to reserve certain rights for themselves.

By contrast, in the *St. Catherine's Milling* case of 1886, the Canadian judiciary signalled its unwillingness to adopt a similar premise, a premise recognizing that the historical realities which gave rise to American Indian legal doctrines were equally applicable to Canada and its First Nations. What passes for Canadian legal doctrine is a racist doctrine which holds at its core the notion that Indians either do not exist as human beings or that they are too primitive, uncivilized and savage to have formed political communities capable of asserting sovereign rights over the territories they occupied.

Such a doctrine, under the name *Lebensraum*, was implemented by Nazi Germany as justification for the lands it attempted to take over in Europe. Such a doctrine was viewed as justifiable by the South African government and judiciary under apartheid. But a doctrine of this kind is clearly at variance with the constitutional values adopted by Canada in 1982. It is in conflict with Canada's commitments as a signatory to various international human rights conventions. It is contrary to Canada's undertakings to the United Nations for eradicating colonialism. Indeed, this doctrine is a criminal breach of international law and an affront to fundamental human decency.

Yet this doctrine continues to ground the thinking of Canadian policy-makers in the approaches they design to dealing with the question of Indian Treaties. That is why, at a fundamental level, the issues regarding Treaties have not moved much beyond the level of thinking evident in the 1969 White Paper.

Both the legal and the political communities in Canada need to move away from the racist premise upon which they presently stand before any measurable breakthrough can occur on the issues of Treaties and Treaty rights. The *Report of the Royal Commission on Aboriginal Peoples* includes some useful recommendations which could serve to ground a political and legal initiative away from the racist presumptions governing the current Canadian approach. Unfortunately, there has been no indication that the Canadian political and legal communities are prepared to pay heed to those particular recommendations.

The issue of "Indian" and "Metis" identity continues to be a contentious issue in Canada, particularly with regard to changes that have occurred since 1969 in the federal laws governing Indian status and in the self-description employed by each of the Indian First Nations and the Metis.

The Metis, having secured express constitutional recognition as Aboriginal peoples in the 1982 constitutional changes, have yet to sort out many issues related to how their citizens are to be recognized by the governments of the country.

Most First Nation citizens now identify themselves more clearly as citizens of a particular First Nation rather than adopting the term "Indian." Indian communities more generally refer to themselves as members of specific First Nations.

Governments and parliamentary committees now describe those formerly referred to as "Indians" as being "Aboriginal peoples," thus lumping all Aboriginal peoples together under one description. That approach raises concerns among many First Nations, since it appears to represent one more attempt on the part of Canadian governments to avoid recognition of Indian First Nations as unique and distinct nations. The changes in terminology belie the fact that the core issues underlying the question of "identity" have yet to be resolved.

The Indian Act, amended in 1985 ostensibly to redress gender and racial discrimination, has created its own host of new identities, and with them new problems. Under the amendments, individual First Nation citizens continue to be described as "Indians," and the Indian Act's original definition of "Indian" stays the same. Legally, it is now more difficult for an Indian to enfranchise. With the enactment of Bill C-31, it is now legally possible for "Indians," particularly Indian women, to regain status previously lost through the former provisions of the Indian Act. But for ordinary folk, the changes have to date been nothing more than smoke and mirrors.

The 1985 amendments to the Indian Act created a new class of Indians. These are persons who meet the legal requirements to be recognized as "status Indians" but do not meet the requirements to be legally considered members of an existing Indian band or reserve. In addition, there are some persons who meet the requirements to be recognized both as Indians and as members of an existing band but who, because of the Indian Act band-control provisions, cannot become members of a band or reserve. The result is a legal hocus pocus in which recovering "status" has little or no meaning.

For some people, particularly those who have died in the legal limbo created by the 1985 amendments, the result has been bitter and tragic. Having recovered their Indian status, they discovered that they remained exiles, unable to exercise the rights inherent in their regained status, unable to return to their communities of origin, and unable to create new communities through which they could exercise their Aboriginal and Treaty rights. For these individuals, the promise contained in the Charter of Rights and Freedoms, the constitutional entrenchment of Aboriginal and Treaty rights, and the Indian Act amendments remained empty unto their graves. For many, the changes are a betrayal of and a fraudulent misrepresentation of the hope and benefits which were promised to them by Canada and its governments. Many Aboriginal individuals continue to live in the legal limbo created by the 1985 amendments to the Indian Act.

White attitudes towards the question of "Indian identity" also remain fundamentally unchanged today. True, Canada has adopted a more multicultural approach to its policies and appears to have ingrained this as a basic constitutional value. Yet when it comes to "Indians," the federal government continues to insist, in its comprehensive claims policy and its comprehensive claims settlements, that "Indians" must give up or extinguish their rights and identities as "First Nations" in order to embrace new municipal-like identities. These new entities, while perhaps retaining the aura of Indian beads, paint and blankets, would in essence become no more than slightly glorified municipalities, with their citizens becoming just like other Canadians.

When *The Unjust Society* was first published, some clergy reacted with horror to the things I wrote regarding residential schools. One nun had the audacity to tell me that I was an "ungrateful savage" who did not appreciate the sacrifices made by the clergy who gave up their lives "to educate you poor Indians."

An Elder who has since passed on told me he could not understand why there was such a negative reaction from some quarters. In his view, there was much more to be said about the residential school experience. Time has shown that the Elder was correct. Canadians are only now becoming aware of the many horrors experienced by First Nation children in the residential schools. As a result of litigation, this dark part of Canada's history is beginning to emerge. In addition, more information is being made public through books, personal testimonies and the exhaustive study on the matter conducted by the Royal Commission on Aboriginal Peoples. Only now are many First Nation persons able to talk about the pain, suffering and humiliation they experienced as children and young adults, and about the effect their experiences have had on them and their communities.

Some First Nation persons maintain, despite the information now emerging, that they on the whole had good experiences and have good memories from their time at the residential schools. Except in rare cases, it is difficult to see how that can be so, particularly when the personal testimonies and the mountain of documentation now available make very clear that these schools were nothing less than state-sponsored programs of cultural genocide aimed at Indian First Nations. They were an integral component of a systematic, intergenerational, state-planned program of brainwashing aimed at removing "the Indian" from the minds and souls of Indian children.

Both the government and the churches responsible have moved to try to limit their potential legal liabilities with regard to operation of the residential schools. But what has not yet emerged is any real understanding of the cumulative effects of these programs and the relationship they bear to the ongoing problems so clearly identified by the *Report of the Royal Commission on Aboriginal Peoples* and a myriad of other bodies.

Some young people now ask how such a thing could have happened in Canada. The answer seems to me fairly straightforward. When a state arrogates unto itself the power to deny to a group of individuals the existence of their humanity, it gives itself absolute power to do as it wants with those individuals. When a state is able through its laws to say that certain human beings are not persons under the law, it removes those persons from the civil and human rights protections extended to those it does recognize as persons under its laws. The result is that the human beings without these protections are treated as animals, as objects of experimentation, as receptacles for abuse—in short, as disposable objects.

Canada created such laws, and because its courts and its citizens viewed Indians as primitive savages, its actions were sanctioned by its legal system and supported by its citizenry.

The policies adopted by Canada over the years with regard to Indians are not different from the rationale employed by Nazi Germany in its implementation of what it called the "Final Solution." Some Jewish people may feel offended by this comparison to the Holocaust, which they justifiably see as a contemporary example of unspeakable horror and injustice. Yet when one considers the scale on which the Americas were depopulated of their original inhabitants and the atrocities that Indian Nations encountered at the hands of Europeans, the parallel is unavoidable. Residential schools represented only one element of a continuing campaign by Europeans in the "New World" to destroy its original inhabitants. In this sense, the horrors experienced by Indian Nations were no less than those experienced by others.

While many Canadian and First Nation peoples may take some comfort from the fact that the residential schools have by and large ceased to exist, it is premature to write off the experience as a thing of the past.

The damage perpetuated by these schools continues to have an impact on the lives of First Nation peoples and on their communities. Because of the silent pain which has been borne by First Nation individuals and the desire of churches and governments to keep the issue under the rug, the nature and character of the long-term damage perpetuated by the residential schools on Aboriginal communities and Aboriginal individuals remain to be carefully identified and clearly understood. Until that is done, it will not be possible to identify the kinds of action required to undo this damage. Without such an understanding, healing, reconciliation and reparation cannot occur. Carefully framed or couched apologies will continue to ring hollow as just one more example of the White man speaking with a forked tongue.

The emergence of these residential school experiences brings out other matters that need to be addressed more clearly within First Nation communities and the Canadian community in general. While it is true that the residential schools have ceased to exist, the legal authority and power of the state over Indian children continues unchanged. They have reemerged in another form. Under Canadian law, the state— through provincial government powers and laws—still claims the right and the power to apprehend First Nation children and, once it apprehends them, to determine "the best interests of the child." This power, though now exercised by a different state agency, is no different from the power used by churches and government agencies to remove First Nation children from their families and put them into the residential schools of the past. Only now, these children are removed either to private families or to other government institutions. The results so far, from a First Nation perspective, are not dissimilar to those arising from residential school experiences.

Canadians ought to know better by now. They ought to know that never, never again should Canada and its governments be allowed to arrogate unto themselves the power to decide what is in the best interests of Indian children. They should ensure that the sole right and primacy of First Nation authority and jurisdiction in this sphere is legally recognized and respected.

As a matter of fundamental principle, Canadians should recognize and accept the fact that First Nations and First Nation families possess and are entitled to possess the primary and sole authority to decide what is in the best interests of their children. This principle should be reflected in legally enforceable fundamental rights and protections for First Nation children—rights and protections binding upon all levels of government, including First Nation governments. The principle should, at its core, recognize that First Nation children possess the God-given birthright to grow up as First Nation persons, to be raised in their own languages and in their own cultures and in their own traditions. If Aboriginal and Treaty rights do not mean at least these things, what do they mean?

In my view, legal recognition of this birthright is the only way to stop importing into the present the problems which occurred in the past.

As I have outlined, much has changed, but much more remains the same. Yet I would be remiss if I did not point out the significant developments that have occurred in many regions of Canada where First Nations and Aboriginal peoples have been successful in assuming economic and political control of their lives.

Education is one area in which political change since 1969 has been real and measurable. In many regions of Canada, Indian student achievement has been accelerated by the assumption of educational control by Indian First Nations. While many problems still have to be ironed out, the development and implementation of policies guaranteeing First Nations educational control has resulted in a dramatic increase in the number of First Nation students in university undergraduate and graduate programs. While one might rightly point out that in proportionate terms we have not yet reached equivalency with the general population, the increase when viewed over the last thirty years is nothing less than astronomical. Today, there are an increasing number of postsecondary institutions under First Nation control and direction. First Nation educational bodies are also increasingly taking a lead role in establishing partnerships with existing universities in a variety of subject areas: dentistry, business, forestry, and so on.

In the economic sphere, new initiatives by governments, First Nations and the private sector have demonstrated that economic progress by First Nations is not only possible but achievable. In some areas, the transfer of program and governance control to First Nations has created increased employment opportunities within First Nation communities.

Either because of their natural resources or because of claims settlements, many First Nation communities have established successful

business enterprises and created a solid economic presence. For example, where there were no Indian-controlled financial institutions at the
time this book was written, there are now a number of Aboriginal-
controlled financial institutions across Canada. In 1969, there was no
economic initiative that enabled First Nations to engage in both the
public and the private sectors. Today, some of the initiatives undertaken
by the Federation of Saskatchewan Indian Nations bear watching. The
government of Saskatchewan and the Federation of Saskatchewan
Indian Nations have agreed to commence discussions on revenue
resource sharing. Within the Treaty regions of Canada, this is the first
initiative of its kind. The principle was apparent in the arrangements
that the parties entered into in relation to gambling, and these arrangements have been productive for both parties. Nothing pleased me more
than to read a front-page article in the Saskatoon *Star Phoenix* stating
that Indian-controlled casinos had outperformed government-controlled
casinos. Irrespective of the nature of the enterprise, what this demonstrated in my view is the fact that, given the opportunity, First Nations
and First Nation entrepreneurs can perform as well as if not better than
their non-Aboriginal counterparts.

There is still a long way to go in the economic area, however. In many
regions of Canada, First Nations are still excluded from participating in
and benefiting from resource development activities in their traditional
territories. There have been visible changes in material terms, be it in
physical facilities or in the construction of quality homes in many First
Nation communities. Yet these changes have not kept pace with First
Nation population growth. Many reserve communities are too small to
sustain their growing populations, with the result that increasing numbers of First Nation peoples are found in urban areas rather than in their
home communities.

Another change that I did not anticipate in 1969 was the acknowledgement by some churches that they had been mistaken in their previous condemnation of First Nation spirituality. Some have issued
apologies for their mistakes and sought to make amends. Much more
needs to be done in this area, where ongoing, meaningful dialogue is
required between the Christian community and traditional First Nation
Elders. And much work remains to be done, within First Nation communities to allow us to understand more fully and completely the central teachings emanating from the ways, practices and institutions given

to our peoples by our Creator. This task is difficult, for it requires us to undo the years and years of brainwashing that our peoples have experienced. It is a task that falls primarily on First Nation peoples, but it is a task that need not be solely ours.

In the thirty years since *The Unjust Society* was first published, my gratitude and admiration for the sacrifices, tenacity, courage and decency of our past Aboriginal leaders have only increased. In the chapter in this book entitled "Quiet Revolution," I describe the beginnings of a national body to represent Indian First Nations in Canada. As with any political movement, the political structures have changed and evolved. At the time, this political movement was focussed on securing gains for individual First Nation citizens, and both the national organization and its provincial affiliates were structured in ways not dissimilar to those of some labour unions or civil rights organizations.

Since that time, there has been a transition. If I were to characterize the change, I would suggest that, as these organizations achieved a measure of success in securing fundamental rights for individual Aboriginal citizens, the initiative shifted to securing the country's recognition of their collective rights, most particularly contemporary Canadian acknowledgement and recognition of the fact that Indians possess unique and distinct political communities.

This shift can be seen in the ways Indian organizations have transformed themselves. For example, the corporate structure of the National Indian Brotherhood was replaced by the Assembly of First Nations. The AFN's name conveyed the message that it represented First Nations coming together as nations, and its structure was constituted to reflect its changed orientation. In this approach, the organization began moving towards a model not unlike that of the United Nations, a body bringing under one roof a broad-ranging group of independent nations. The provincial organizations have transformed themselves in similar ways.

This national collective orientation has enabled First Nation leaders to move the Canadian/Aboriginal political dialogue to a new level. If nothing else, the Charlottetown Accord signalled the new plane on which the political dialogue would be carried out. This change is partly attributable to the constitutional processes in which First Nations have generally participated, but in the main it reflects a perspective long advanced by traditional peoples from all the Indian Nations.

Unheard of in the Canadian/First Nation dialogue of 1969, the dialogue of today is about how First Nation governments can be accommodated as a constitutional third order of government in Canada. This shift is in large part a result of the efforts put forth by the Aboriginal leadership of Canada and is reflective of the institutional and organizational changes which have occurred in Indian country. The federal government now recognizes the inherent right of self-government as an existing constitutional right. The *Report of the Royal Commission on Aboriginal Peoples* outlines different options that might be considered in implementing this right.

This "inherent rights" agenda is at a very preliminary stage, and it is too early to determine the directions that it will take. What is clear, however, is that fundamental change has occurred in the political framework of First Nations, and our successes have gone far beyond the wildest expectations of our Elders, particularly in 1969, when we were fighting for our survival. Those of us who were then participants still shudder at the thought of how perilously close we came to seeing the termination of Indian First Nations in Canada.

The title of Chapter 16 in this book, "When the Curtain Comes Down," referred to the external and internal isolation First Nations faced at the time. Tremendous steps have been taken since then in breaking down our isolation from one another. In addition, with the creation of the World Council of Indigenous Peoples and the representation of Non-Governmental Organizations—NGOs—at the United Nations and other world bodies, Indian First Nations have made huge gains towards breaking down the isolation from the international community brought about by European colonialism.

Further contributing to our emergence on the world scene has been the recent practice of the federal government and the Assembly of First Nations in ensuring the presence of First Nation representatives in at least some of Canada's trade and international delegations. While much remains to be done in this arena, over a thirty-year period the curtain has begun to come down in many noticeable ways.

Yet the question posed thirty years ago about whether Canada would see a cultural renaissance or civil disorder is as valid today as it was then. We seem no closer today to a definitive answer.

The enlightened segment of Canadian society appears willing to break away from its past colonial mindset, enabling it to welcome and embrace First Nations as unique and distinct political communities who are entitled to realize their right to self-determination within the constitutional framework of Canada. There is, however, an increasingly vocal and well-organized movement which embraces as its core value the philosophy contained in the 1969 White Paper—a philosophy which argues that "equality" requires Indians to give up their special identity, their homelands and their unique status before they can be embraced as "Canadian citizens." If this philosophy gains ascendancy in Canada, the result can only be increasing discord and growing social and political conflict.

—Harold Cardinal
Sucker Creek Cree First Nation
April 1999

The Buckskin Curtain

The Indian-Problem Problem

The history of Canada's Indians is a shameful chronicle of the white man's disinterest, his deliberate trampling of Indian rights and his repeated betrayal of our trust. Generations of Indians have grown up behind a buckskin curtain of indifference, ignorance and, all too often, plain bigotry. Now, at a time when our fellow Canadians consider the promise of the Just Society, once more the Indians of Canada are betrayed by a programme which offers nothing better than cultural genocide.

The new Indian policy promulgated by Prime Minister Pierre Elliott Trudeau's government, under the auspices of the Honourable Jean Chrétien, minister of Indian Affairs and Northern Development, and Deputy Minister John A. MacDonald, and presented in June 1969 is a thinly disguised programme of extermination through assimilation. For the Indian to survive, says the government in effect, he must become a good little brown white man. The Americans to the south of us used to have a saying: "The only good Indian is a dead Indian." The MacDonald-Chrétien doctrine would amend this but slightly to, "The only good Indian is a non-Indian."

The federal government, instead of acknowledging its legal and moral responsibilities to the Indians of Canada and honouring the treaties that the Indians signed in good faith, now proposes to wash its hands of Indians entirely, passing the buck to the provincial governments.

Small wonder that in 1969, in the one hundred and second year of Canadian confederation, the native people of Canada look back on generations of accumulated frustration under conditions which can only be described as colonial, brutal and tyrannical, and look to the future with the gravest of doubts.

Torrents of words have been spoken and written about Indians since the arrival of the white man on the North American continent. Endless columns of statistics have been compiled. Countless programmes have been prepared for Indians by non-Indians. Faced with society's general indifference and a massive accumulation of misdirected, often insincere efforts, the greatest mistake the Indian has made has been to remain so long silent.

As an Indian writing about a situation I am living and experiencing in common with thousands of our people it is my hope that this book will open the eyes of the Canadian public to its shame. In these pages I hope to cut through bureaucratic doubletalk to show what it means to be an Indian in Canada. I intend to document the betrayals of our trust, to show step by step how a dictatorial bureaucracy has eroded our rights, atrophied our culture and robbed us of simple human dignity. I will expose the ignorance and bigotry that has impeded our progress, the eighty years of educational neglect that have hobbled our young people for generations, the gutless politicians who have knowingly watched us sink in the quicksands of apathy and despair and have failed to extend a hand.

I hope to point a path to radical change that will admit the Indian with restored pride to his rightful place in the Canadian heritage, that will enable the Indian in Canada at long last to realize his dreams and aspirations and find his place in Canadian society. I will challenge our fellow Canadians to help us; I will warn them of the alternatives.

I challenge the Honourable Mr. Trudeau and the Honourable Mr. Chrétien to reexamine their unfortunate policy, to offer the Indians of Canada hope instead of despair, freedom instead of frustration, life in the Just Society instead of cultural annihilation.

It sometimes seems to Indians that Canada shows more interest in preserving its rare whooping cranes than its Indians. And Canada, the Indian notes, does not ask its cranes to become Canada geese. It just wants to preserve them as whooping cranes. Indians hold no grudge against the big, beautiful, nearly extinct birds, but we would like to know how they managed their deal. Whooping cranes can remain whooping cranes, but Indians are to become brown white men. The contrast in the situation is an insult to our people. Indians have aspirations, hopes and dreams, but becoming white men is not one of them.

Indifference? Indians have witnessed the growing concern of Canadians over racial strife in the United States. We have watched the justifiably indignant reaction of fellow Canadians to the horrors of starvation in Biafra. Television has brought into our homes the sad plight of the Vietnamese, has intensified the concern of Canadians about the role of our neighbour country in the brutal inhumanity of war. The Unitarian Service Committee reminds us of the starving conditions of hundreds of thousands of Asians. Canadian urbanites have walked blisters on their feet and fat off their rumps to raise money for underdeveloped countries outside Canada.

We do not question the concern of Canadians about such problems. We do question how sincere or how deep such concern may be when Canadians ignore the plight of the Indian or Métis or Eskimo in their own country. There is little knowledge of native circumstances in Canada and even less interest. To the native one fact is apparent—the average Canadian does not give a damn.

The facts are available, dutifully compiled and clucked over by a handful of government civil servants year after year. Over half the Indians of Canada are jobless year after year. Thousands upon thousands of native people live in housing which would be condemned in any advanced society on the globe. Much of the housing has no inside plumbing, no running water, no electricity. A high percentage of the native peoples of Canada never get off welfare. This is the way it is, not in Asia or Africa but here in Canada. The facts are available; a Sunday drive to the nearest reserve will confirm them as shocking reality.

Bigotry? The problem grows worse, not better. A survey by the Canadian Corrections Association, entitled *Indians and the Law*, reveals some of the problems that the native person faces in the area of prejudice and discrimination. The survey reports bluntly: "Underlying all problems associated with Indians and Eskimo in this country are the prejudice and discrimination they meet in the attitudes of non-Indians. The result is a conviction on the part of the Indians and Eskimo that they are not really part of the dominant Canadian society and that their efforts to better themselves will fail because they do not have an even chance."

Probably the most perceptive statement of the report observes: "Few non-Indians will admit to feelings of prejudice against the Indian and Eskimo people because such views are no longer acceptable, but the façade often vanishes when problems arise."

Many Canadians, however, have always claimed and continue to assert that Canada has little racial difficulty. Statements of this nature are just so much uninformed nonsense.

In any area where there is a concentration of native people there exists racial tension. Urban centres with their multiplicity of attractions and opportunities are drawing more and more natives who come in hope and stay in misery. These migrants, with little financial security, all too often with insufficient job training and nearly always with terribly inadequate knowledge of white mores, inevitably jam into ghettos, increasing not only their own problems but those of the city. The people of the city answer with bigotry, wrongly attributing the problem to colour or race rather than to any inadequacy of opportunity and social response.

As Indian people attempt to organize and as Indian leaders become more vocal and articulate, the shades of bigotry which now appear in pastel will show up in more vivid colours. People who are tolerant of a problem which hasn't touched them are put to the test when the problem moves next door.

As an ethnocentric society, the Canadian non-Indian society puts its own peer group at the centre of all things desirable and rates all other cultures accordingly. It is an assumption, quite often becoming a conviction, that the values, the ways of life, the whole culture of one's own group must be superior to those of others. Tell a person long enough and often enough that he is inferior, and likely he will eventually accept the false image you thrust upon him.

An Indian leader in the Northwest Territories, asked why his people couldn't do a certain job for themselves, wisely and sadly observed, "They could, but they have been told for so long by the white man that they can't that now they don't think they can." Indians long have been victims of this sort of conscious and unconscious downgrading pressure from the non-Indian.

Ignorance? It thrives on the incestuous mating of indifference and bigotry and in turn breeds more of the same. Ignorance is irretrievably locked in with prejudice. How often have you heard a white man say, "Indians are lousy workers," or, "Indians are shiftless" or "dirty" or "lazy," or, "Indians are drunken bums"? I have seen in numerous cities across the country non-Indians engaged in excessive drinking, making drunken fools of themselves. In these circumstances, what do you hear? "Well, isn't he having a ball," or "He's just letting his hair down," or, perhaps, "Boy, isn't he a real swinger!" Let native people be seen in similar conditions and what do you get? The comments are more in the nature of epithets: "Worthless drunks!" or "Drunken bums!"

This double standard has stereotyped the native people as a whole as people who can't handle liquor. More damaging is the fact that similar double standards are applied to nearly every aspect of native life. Typically, the Indians-can't-hold-their-liquor theory is inexcusably used by church groups or church leaders to try to force governments to accept the churches' views on liquor. And employers, like the churches, use this stereotype as a lever against government enforcement of fair employment standards. Let a white man get drunk and miss a day of work ... his boss may fire him, but he gets another white man for the job. He doesn't say, "All white workers are drunken bums and too shiftless to hold a job." If the Indian misses a day, the entire race is condemned and categorized as no good; the next worker hired is not likely to be an Indian.

If more of these church groups, more of these employers and more of the other pressure groups who make opportune use of this handy double standard were honest with themselves and with government, they would quit using the Indian as an excuse to foist their own beliefs on the rest of society.

It can be argued that ignorance in some segments of society is understandable if not excusable, but ignorance at higher levels is neither. Political leaders must have, at the very least, a working knowledge of the particular constituencies they represent. They must know the people who elected them to represent their viewpoints; they must know the problems, the needs, the desires of "their" people. Particularly is this true when a politician is named to higher office, for example, a ministry.

Ministers of the crown have a large bureaucracy available to inform, advise and help them in the discharge of their responsibilities. They have almost endless resources upon which to draw. Nor are they dependent entirely upon such official and hired help. Their constituents also, for the most part, have resources. They have their own organizations or lobbies; they may have financial resources which can be utilized and will most often be respected. They have the means and the talent to present to the minister their own viewpoints and they can bring sufficient pressure to make certain "their" minister or "their" representative listens. Furthermore, the news media, because of their responsibility to look at both sides of the picture and to bring balanced views to bear on current problems, help elected representatives of the people discharge their duties properly and in an informed manner.

All of this theoretically works fine as a system of checks and balances, providing the necessary background knowledge and understanding of a situation to ensure proper and fair legislation ... except that none of the above applies to Indians in Canada.

Throughout the hundreds of years of the Indian-government relationship, political leaders responsible for matters relating to Indians have been outstanding in their ignorance of the native people and remarkable in their insensitivity to the needs and aspirations of the Indians in Canada. More often than not, government people simply do not know what they are doing, and if they show any evidence of caring, it usually is in direct proportion to political pressure and political expediency at the time.

The question of paramount importance in the minds of successive ministers responsible for Indian Affairs appears to have been and to remain the defence of the gross ineptitude of their department. Any attempt to uncover the actual state of affairs and do the necessary housecleaning appears to have been either beyond them or of no interest to them.

Two factors play a part in the seemingly endless state of ignorance displayed by most federal politicians about native people. Too many are content to close their minds to any but the stereotype images so easy to pick up in Canada. They make little or no effort to go to the people and find out firsthand what is really happening. Secondly, until very recently, the question of Indians had never been a major political issue. The people of Canada simply have not been moved by the problem. Consequently, members of Parliament haven't felt it worth their time to investigate the Indian situation.

Historically, the question of Indians has been one raised by politicians for some purely ulterior motive, perhaps to create an image of social awareness or compassion. The concern has been passing, viable only when the image was politically attractive, usually forgotten as soon as the votes were counted or the winds of change blew from another quarter.

Most politicians and, as far as that goes, most Canadians, tend to plead ignorance as a defence for the inexcusable treatment of the native people of this country. One should keep in mind that ignorance is not acceptable in law as a defence, even in the case of a violated local ordinance, nor is it acceptable in international courts passing judgment on crimes against humanity.

However, even more reprehensible than the man who does not act because he is ignorant is the man who *does* know the situation but fails to act. I can only label this type of performance *gutless*. When I talk of a gutless person, I am talking about a human being who does not have the courage to try to change an unjust situation. I call gutless a person, who, rather than change an indefensible state of affairs, tries to sweep the mess under a rug. I call gutless the politician who stalls, procrastinates and tries to perpetuate the antiquated systems and attitudes which have produced injustice, in order to try to maintain his own positive image. When I look at the existing situation among the natives of Canada, I cannot help but assume we must have a hell of a lot of gutless politicians in this country.

In 1969 it is true that there are some notable exceptions on the political scene: Robert Andras, minister responsible for Housing; Martin O'Connell, a Liberal backbencher from Toronto and a member of the House Standing Committee on Indian Affairs; Gerald Baldwin, a Conservative member from Peace River and Frank Howard, the New Democratic party member from British Columbia. While a few men like these have worked to build up Indian competence and leadership qualities, many more through the years have contributed to a disastrous and calculated programme of leadership destruction.

The white man's government has allowed (worse, urged) its representatives to usurp from Indian peoples our right to make our own decisions and our authority to implement the goals we have set for ourselves. In fact, the real power, the decision-making process and the policy-implementing group, has always resided in Ottawa, in the Department of Indian Affairs and Northern Development. To ensure the complete disorganization of native peoples, Indian leadership over the past years and yet today has been discredited and destroyed. Where this was not possible, the bureaucrats have maintained the upper hand by subjecting durable native leaders to endless exercises in futility, to repeated, pointless reorganizations, to endless barrages of verbal diarrhoea promising never-coming changes.

Indeed, the real tanners of hides for the Buckskin Curtain are these self-same bureaucrats. To gain insight into the Indian problem, a basic understanding of the group of people known as bureaucrats, civil servants or mandarins working in the Department of Indian Affairs and Northern Development (formerly the Indian Affairs Branch of the Department of Citizenship and Immigration) is necessary.

These faceless people in Ottawa, a comparatively small group, perpetually virtually unknown, have sat at their desks eight hours a day, five days a week, for over a century, and decided just about everything that will ever happen to a Canadian Indian. They have laid down the policy, the rules, the regulations on all matters affecting native peoples. They have decided where our sons will go to school, near home or hopelessly far from home; they have decided what houses will be built on what reserves for what Indians and whether they may have inside or outside toilets; they have decided what types of social or economic development will take place and where and how it will be controlled. If you are a treaty Indian, you've never made a move without these guys, these bureaucrats, these civil servants at their desks in their new office tower in Ottawa saying "yes" ... or "no."

And, you know something? It would almost be funny if it weren't so pathetic. In the latter part of 1968, a government official suggested publicly that the mandarins in Ottawa would probably not even recognize an Indian if they met one on the street.

These are the people who make the decisions, the policies, the plans and programmes by which we live, decisions made in almost total isolation from the Indians in Canada. Their ignorance of the people whose lives and destinies they so routinely control perpetuates the stereotype image they have developed of the native people.

Through generations of justifying their positions to the Canadian public and to Canada's political leaders, the bureaucrats within the department have come to believe their own propaganda. They have fostered an image of Indians as a helpless people, an incompetent people and an apathetic people in order to increase their own importance and to stress the need for their own continued presence.

Most of their action stems from their naïveté and a genuine belief that their solutions are necessary to ensure the survival of Indians. For the most part they are not really evil men. They have evolved no vicious plots intentionally to subjugate the Indian people. The situation for the Indian people, as bad as it is, has resulted largely from good intentions, however perverted, of civil servants within the Department of Indian Affairs. However, one cannot forget the direction usually taken by roads paved with nothing but good intentions.

Small wonder that the report on *Indians and the Law* notes: "Many non-Indians believe that nothing better can be expected from the descendants of Canada's original people, and many Indians and Eskimo oblige by acting in a way that confirms this expectation."

I have talked with many Indian people. I have had the opportunity to discuss our situation as a people with affluent Indians who have it made and with Indians living in the worst state of deprivation. I have met my fellow Indians of all generations, in all walks of life and from nearly every part of Canada.

Always I find that as Indian people, we share hopes for a better Canada, a better future and a better deal. We share hopes that Canadian society will accept us as we are and will listen to what we have to say.

One of the most difficult challenges our people face comes with this question of acceptance by non-Indian society. Certainly it means that on both sides we must change misconceptions about each other. It means that we must have the intelligence and the courage to set aside the old stereotypes on both sides. It means that we must change negative attitudes, shrug off bigotry, overcome the accumulated effects of generations of isolation from each other. It means honest-to-God intellectual and emotional effort by Indians and non-Indians.

Acceptance of the Indian in non-Indian society must mean acceptance as an individual in his own right, as a fellow human being. I emphasize the need for acceptance on an individual or personal basis. As members of a minority group we sometimes are bemused by the attitude of non-Indian people who meet us. Sometimes we literally can see the expression on their faces saying, "How do I approach this Indian? Can I go over and say hello? Will he be offended if I do this or say that? How should I act?" No problem, really. Be yourself. If you are a snob, you aren't going to make it with us anyhow. If you are a phoney, we're going to sense it. If you are okay, then there will be no problem. Just don't try to fake it. Be yourself. Now and then Indians run into a situation where a non-Indian makes his presence obnoxious by attempting to show that he feels you are no different than he is. He may think this is a great compliment, but you know damned well you *are* different from him—and, as often as not, you are glad of it.

Is it, then, too much to ask that we be accepted by the larger Canadian society as individuals in our own right, who can and will work with members of that larger society without first being required to become brown white men or white-washed brown men?

Talking and listening have been one-way streets with white men and Indians. Until very recently white men have expected Indians to do all the listening. Indians, on the other hand, have felt that the white man just couldn't shut up long enough to listen. For many years now our people have talked about what concerned them most, have suggested solutions to our problems as we see them, have talked generally about our hopes for a better future. Some have talked articulately and with eloquence, some less lucidly; some have spoken with great intensity and emotion, others with objectivity and almost passively. But all talk, brilliant or dull, visionary or cautiously realistic, remains futile when the people you talk to simply won't listen. We want the white man to shut up and listen to us, really listen for a change. Some Canadians listen but they wish to hear Indians say only what white people want to hear. They like to hear an Indian tell them what a good job government is doing and how the lowly Indian would have vanished if not for the white man's help. Such people quit listening when an Indian tries to tell them the hard facts of Indian life in Canada.

The Indian people are now impatient with the verbal games that have been played. We want the beginnings of a real and purposeful dialogue with non-Indian people and government representatives in order to get on with the business of solving some of the most basic difficulties that we face. When we enter into a dialogue, we wish to have the respect and the courtesy of the non-Indian society in their recognition that we are talking sense, that we have the intelligence and capacity to judge for ourselves what is good or bad for us. When we offer suggestions, we expect those suggestions to be given the attention they deserve, instead of the usual brush-off. Are you familiar with that brush-off? It goes, "Well, boys, what you have to say is good and you must be commended for the intelligence you have shown through your extremely good presentation," and, subsequently, the inevitable, "but we know your problems and what should be done, and we're certain that you will be pleased with our carefully considered decisions."

We want to be heard as reasonable, thinking people, able to identify with our own problems and to present rational solutions. We want to be treated as human beings with the dignity and equality we feel is our right. We ask the non-Indian society to wake up to things the way they are, to see us as a people with needs, emotions and untapped potential. These are the hopes of the present generation of Indian leaders. Surely these cannot be unreasonable hopes. They must not be.

We listen when Canadian political leaders talk endlessly about strength in diversity for Canada, but we understand they are talking primarily about the French Canadian fact in Canada. Canadian Indians feel, along with other minorities, that there is a purpose and a place for us in a Canada which accepts and encourages diversified human resources. We like the idea of a Canada where all cultures are encouraged to develop in harmony with one another, to become part of the great mosaic. We are impatient for the day when other Canadians will accord the Indian the recognition implied in this vision of Canada.

The vast majority of our people are committed to the concept of Canadian unity and to the concept of participation in that unity. The Indians of Canada surely have as great a commitment to Canada, if not a greater one, than even the most patriotic-sounding political leaders. More truly than it can be said of anyone else, it is upon this land that our heritage, our past and our identity originates. Our commitment to Canada exists because of our belief that we have a responsibility to do all we can to ensure that our country is a nation with which we can proudly identify.

To fulfill our dreams for participation in the greatness of Canada, we must be able to contribute to Canada. We invite our white brothers to realize and acknowledge that the Indian in Canada has already made a considerable contribution to the greatness of our country, that the Indian has played a significant role in Canadian history. Our people look on with concern when the Canadian government talks about "the two foundling peoples" without giving recognition to the role played by the Indian even before the founding of a nation-state known as Canada.

However, Canada's Indians look to the future as the greatest period for participation. Our contribution will be based upon what we are as a people, upon what, as a culture, Indian society will add to the mosaic and upon what we can accomplish as individuals to add to our country's total potential.

Here there is a lack, glaringly obvious. Our people lack the skills through which we might best contribute as individuals. If the Indian receives no training as a doctor then he cannot add to Canada's potential in medical advances. If he does not acquire the skills of a politician, he cannot hope to advance Canada politically. The Indian people must realize their greatest contributions to Canada's potential through whatever skills they may be able to add to Canada's pool of know-how. This is why Indians include in their aspirations better training in skills at all working levels, from professional to technical, to make it possible for each of us to work with our fellow Canadians so that the sum total of our efforts as Canadians results in the growth and expansion of the land we call our home.

No one realizes better than the Indian that the road ahead is long and hard going. There exist more than two thousand reserves across Canada, situated in every geographical area of our immense country, some actually within the boundaries of major cities (in Vancouver, Winnipeg and

Toronto), some deep in the underdeveloped northern wildernesses, many isolated not only from the mainstream of society but from one another. The needs and the problems of Indians living in such diverse circumstances vary widely and, of course, the environment influences greatly their desires and ambitions.

The language barrier has isolated our people as truly as the geographical barrier. There are eleven different major language groups among the Indians of Canada with scores of dialects changing from band to band. Only recently has English become universal enough among Indians to serve as a medium of communication. And, even today, the most articulate (in English) Indian will confess readily that he still feels more at home in his mother tongue.

Nationwide Indian unity represents a dream long held by Indian leaders well aware of the divisive influence of the emphasis upon individual bands and tribes. Only recently, with the growth of strong provincial organizations in turn leading to the creation for the first time of a viable national organization, the National Indian Brotherhood, has this dream shown signs of realization. When our people begin to call themselves Indians instead of Crees or Saulteaux or Mohawks, when intertribal cooperation no longer allows the government to threaten our individual treaties, then we will have the strength of unity, the power to help make some of our other dreams come true.

Canada is an enormous country. Even within a single province such as Alberta, conditions vary so widely from reserve to reserve that common needs, aspirations and goals that can be attributed to the entire Indian people are often difficult to determine.

Perhaps our most persistent dreams stem from our most insistent reality—poverty—the one reality most Indians share. Perhaps because the Indian people face the most difficult and demoralizing situation in Canada, our aspirations are the more intense. We face the greatest challenge and, at the same time, the greatest threat.

Indians gladly accept the challenge—to become participating Canadians, to take a meaningful place in the mainstream of Canadian society. But we remain acutely aware of the threat—the loss of our Indian identity, our place as distinct, identifiable Canadians.

However idealistic some Indian dreams may be, there remain everyday hopes that come right down to earth. Indians are like anyone else. We look around and see a very affluent society. Just like our non-Indian neighbours, we want a share, a new car, a well-built home, television.

These represent surface things, but it hurts deeply to see the affluence of our country and not be allowed to benefit from it. We want better education, a better chance for our children and the option to choose our own pathway in life. If we are to be part of the Canadian mosaic, then we want to be colourful red tiles, taking our place where red is both needed and appreciated.

Our people wish to become involved in all aspects of the professional community, but how many Indian doctors, Indian lawyers, Indian community planners, Indian engineers, artist, writers, professors do you know in Canada? While we see the white society training its young people for life in the professional and technological world of the space age, we find the government attempting to train our people in skills that have not been required since the Industrial Revolution.

If we as a people are to assume a purposeful role in our own lives, if we are to become truly involved in today's and tomorrow's society, then we must be given the opportunity of controlling our own future. Indians resent eternal overprotection. How can we take our place in the world, ever hope to make the right choices, if we are denied the opportunity to choose at every remote chance of peril? Have no white men ever failed? Have no white men ever risen above failure, the wiser for the experience?

An aspiration that seems to puzzle and disturb the white man remains common to every Indian I have ever talked to who is on welfare. This aspiration is simply to get off relief. You'll never find a prouder Indian than one who can say, "I've never been on welfare." The fact that such a high percentage of Indians are on welfare at any given moment only sharpens the point. Indians realize that social assistance is part of the white man's world, that many white families must accept welfare. Indians accept the fact that now and then circumstances may dictate to any man that he must accept temporary help in clothing and feeding his family but, and this seems to surprise the white man, the Indian by nature finds acceptance of welfare demeaning. It is not so much the giving as the implication. When that man looks at you as he hands over the check and you reach for it, you know what his look means. It means that you aren't man enough to make your own living; it means that you aren't man enough to feed and clothe and house your own wife and children. That's when an Indian hates welfare. That's why a common dream among Indians coast to coast and border to pole is to get off welfare.

We want to get involved, but we have had only a gutful of vague philosophical government commitments to give us opportunities for involvement. To us involvement remains meaningless without the money to make it work. It's just so much Ottawa doubletalk to tell us to go ahead on any programme without proper provision for the financial, human and physical resources that are required. Involvement must mean enough money to enable Indian people to hire the professional consultants and experts necessary, without regard as to whether they are red, white or yellow. It means money to buy equipment and facilities and it means access to years and years of accumulated research documents buried deep in dusty files in the Indian Affairs offices. Only when the government is willing to back up its lip service to the ideal of Indian involvement with the necessary resources will we be able to talk in terms of a meaningful role for Indians in charting a course for our future. Until then, all statements by the federal government about involving Indians are hypothetical exercises, irrelevant, academic and utterly useless to the Indian.

We have charted the difficulties ahead; we know the obstacles. No matter how concerted an effort we make, we realize that many problems will fall only to combined Indian and non-Indian assault. We point out that to begin, some problems must be faced up to as government responsibilities.

One such major problem arises from the refusal of our present Canadian government in its most recent white paper, and of Canadian governments in the past, to honour commitments for treaties signed with the Indians. Coupled closely with this is the unwillingness of successive governments to recognize the aboriginal rights of our people.

Government after government has, in some way or another, vaguely committed itself to native rights but no government, including and particularly the one in power today, has yet committed itself to the simple honesty of fulfilling its obligations to our people as outlined in the treaties. I will deal more fully with the treaty problem in a later chapter, but it can be noted here that as far as the Indians are concerned, there is not one treaty that has not been broken by the white man, not one treaty fulfilled.

Positive steps by the government to fulfill its treaty obligations represent one aspiration common to all Indians. It was for this reason that our people were encouraged by Prime Minister Trudeau's call for the creation of the Just Society. This brief, dazzling flare of hope, however, quickly fizzled when Mr. Trudeau publicly announced that the federal government was not prepared to guarantee aboriginal rights and that the Canadian government considered the Indian treaties an anomaly not to be tolerated in the Just Society.

We will not trust the government with our futures any longer. Now they must listen to and learn from us.

Red Tape

Definitions and Divisions

Canadians worry about their identity. Are they too English? Are they too American? Are they French Canadians or some other kind of hybrid? Indians worry about their identity, too. For the most part they like to think of themselves as Canadians. But there are towns and cities in Canada, in every province of Canada, where an Indian dares not forget his identity as an Indian. There are towns and cities in Canada where a Canadian Indian simply dares not go.

If that seems a shocking statement to the non-Indian, it shocks Indians even more. There are towns and cities in Canada where simply being an Indian means getting a beating. Indians in such towns and cities have even been dragged out of restaurants into the streets and beaten. In such cases an Indian foolish enough to attempt to bring charges finds *himself* charged with creating a disturbance. No citizen is likely to forget his identity under such circumstances.

For the Canadian Indian the question of identity bears heavily on the kind of life a native may lead. Under Canada's mixed-up legal definition, full-blooded Indians may be classed as non-Indian, and full-blooded whites can legally be Indians. The *Indian Act* defines an Indian as "a person who pursuant to this Act registered as an Indian or is entitled to be registered as an Indian." This simplistic legalism, however, eliminates roughly 250,000 native people who, under the American system, would be recognized as Indian.

This *Indian Act* definition has been and continues to be a divisive force among Canada's natives. If you are legally an Indian, then you and your family can live on reserves and are entitled to certain limited rights. No matter how full-blooded you may be, if you are not a legal Indian, you can forget the reserve. You can't live there.

The whole silly bit about who is an Indian and who isn't came about as a result of the treaties. On the Prairies, the native people were given a choice at the time of signing as to the status they wanted. If they chose to be Indians under treaty, native people were promised certain treaty rights, including land on a reserve, perpetual hunting and fishing rights, along with myriad lesser pledges, but they were denied the right to vote or access to liquor.

The alternative was to choose script, a legal piece of paper proclaiming the victim's citizenship, providing a sum of money (it varied in different treaties) and a piece of land (the area varied). This choice gave access to liquor and the vote, the same privileges accorded any citizen of Canada.

If a man chose to give up his Indian status, he never could reclaim it. But if a native chose to become a registered or treaty Indian, he still retained a sort of horrible option. He could enfranchise. This meant and still means that a treaty or registered or legal Indian still could and still can give up his special status by applying to Ottawa for enfranchisement. This remains a pretty drastic decision for an Indian. He gains full citizenship rights, the vote, liquor (which he now can get as an Indian, anyhow) and, in theory, becomes a Canadian like anyone else. But he renounces his Indianness: he loses all treaty or aboriginal rights; he gives up forever his right to membership on a reserve and all title to his portion of resources or reserve land. He cannot return to the reserve to take up residence where the rest of his family, his relatives and his friends live.

If the parents make this choice or if an entire Indian family enfranchises, then the children of that family and all subsequent grandchildren and direct heirs lose forever the right to claim title to being Indians, at least legally. The only exception to this loss of identity occurs in maternal lineage. If any woman, Indian or non-Indian, marries a treaty or registered Indian, she automatically becomes a legal Indian; no matter whether she is red, white, yellow or black, married to a legal Indian she becomes one, too. However, it doesn't work the other way around. If an Indian woman marries a non-Indian man, she automatically forfeits her claim to be an Indian.

Just to make it more confusing, when a white or non-Indian woman becomes by reason of marriage legally an Indian, this does not mean that her children necessarily will be Indian. Under section 12, subsection (a) 4 of the *Indian Act*, effective in the 1970s, a person whose mother and paternal grandmother are non-Indian (except by right of marriage) also loses his claim to be an Indian.

This legal hocus-pocus has created many problems for the younger generation. In some instances, where full-blooded Indian families have for one reason or another enfranchised, they and their children are, in the eyes of the law, non-Indian, Métis or even white—in theory. At the same time, in the case of a white woman marrying a registered Indian, she and her children suddenly, in the eyes of the law, are Indians. Among the younger generation where pride of race once again is growing, Indians in all but the law have found themselves classed as non-Indian no matter how much they want to be Indians, because parents enfranchised. Many young Indians today are being denied their birthright because someone else decided to renounce his legal claims to being Indian. They have no recourse; they never legally can reclaim their birthright.

Stan Daniels, president of the Métis Association of Alberta, puts the problem this way: "The question of my identity is hard for me to understand; on one hand, when I consider myself an Indian, and I say this, the Indian says, 'Who do you think you are: you are nothing but a white man.' And when I consider myself a white man, talk or act like one, the white man says to me, 'Who in the hell do you think you are? You're nothing but a damned Indian.' I am a man caught in the vacuum of two cultures with neither fully accepting me."

Legalities continue to play a divisive role among Canadian Indians. Even among those who have a legal right to be Indian, further classifications complicate the matter. There is, for example, a distinction between treaty Indians and registered Indians. A treaty Indian is one whose ancestors signed a treaty with the representatives of the queen and ceded some land rights to the crown in return for specified rights. Treaties have been signed with Indians in Ontario, Manitoba, Saskatchewan, Alberta and portions of the Northwest Territories. A registered Indian is one whose ancestros signed no treaties, such as Indians in the Maritimes, in Quebec, in portions of the Northwest Territories and in British Columbia, but who did choose under the *Indian Act* to be regarded as legal or registered Indians. Maritimes Indians signed "pacts of friendship" with the representatives of the queen. Many treaty Indians fear that association with Indians from non-treaty areas will jeopardize their claims to their treaty rights, while Indians from the non-treaty areas are concerned that association with treaty Indians will compromise their requests for settlement of aboriginal claims. In some cases, even minor differences between treaties can confuse and worry Indians as to their rights when they intermingle. Treaty Six carries a medicine chest promise, which in present-day usage can be considered the right to paid-up medicare. Treaties Seven and Eight, although the question of medical treatment was promised verbally, never followed through on this issue in writing. A Treaty Six Indian conceivably could lose her claims to medical care by marrying a Treaty Seven man.

Sneakier things than that have come from government offices. In fact, the government, specifically the Department of Indian Affairs and Northern Development, seems to enjoy this divisiveness and even, in many cases, to encourage it. Anything that divides the Indians makes the department stronger. No wonder no Indian in his right mind trusts the department.

Some progress is being made toward unity among Canada's native people, but much work remains to be done to tear down this inner Buckskin Curtain. It is self-definition, not this network of inhuman legalities or the recently proposed alternative of assimilation, that will foster Indian unity. All the legal definitions fail to accomplish one thing—they fail to solve the real, human problem of identity. Identity means as much to an Indian as it does to the Québecois in Trois Rivières or the Icelander in Gimli. Obviously this has no meaning for many people. They are the sort who feel that the only future for the Indian lies in assimilation. Such people see all residents of Canada as Canadians, without regard to ethnic background. As far as we are concerned, these melting-pot advocates don't understand the nature of our country, let alone the nature of the native. To all too many, being Canadian simply means, "white is right," or "be Anglo and you'll be happy," or "be like me and all your problems will vanish."

Other people, both Indian and non-Indian, seem to feel that being Indian means being some sort of relic out of the past, a guy with a feathered headdress and beaded buckskin clothes, a buffalo hunter. They feel that Indianness is a thing of the past, with no relevance today. Indians who feel this way can be spotted quickly. They continually apologize for being Indian. They may be extremely successful in the white man's world, perhaps even in Canadian legislative bodies, but they always apologize for being Indian. You don't hear a man like Lincoln Alexander, MP for Hamilton, apologize for being a Negro.

Such Uncle Tomahawks have a compelling urge to go around telling other Indians to pull up their bootstraps. Once they have it made, they seem to develop a case of very bad memory as to how it was with them on the way up. They lose touch and become blind to the circumstances under which their "brothers" are living. They don't command much respect from their own people for very long. Indians can be fooled once, like anyone else, but don't try it twice.

When I attended a white school, there were very few Indians there. None ever wore articles of Indian apparel. When winter came, I put on my mukluks. Some of the other Indian students came to me and suggested I shouldn't wear them. My mukluks called attention to the fact that I was an Indian. But I continued to wear them, not as any sort of hollow protest and not feeling particularly self-righteous—just warm. The next year more Indian students found the "courage" to wear Indian clothing in which they felt comfortable. By my third year, even the white students who could get them were wearing mukluks.

Now Indian clothing is acceptable. In fact it has become high fashion in some quarters. The only problem now is that an Indian runs the risk of being taken for a hippie if he wears his ordinary clothing.

I wear a buckskin jacket today and have for many years. I wear it first of all because it is one of the most comfortable garments I have, but I also wear it as an example to young Indians. One other reason: I got tired of being asked if I were from China or Japan or India or somewhere like that. I got tired of having people jump to the conclusion that, just because I was educated and could talk like a white man, even though I obviously am not one, that I must be Asian. I wear my buckskin jacket because it says, "I am a Canadian Indian."

For a long time many, many Indians accepted the white man's evaluation of them as a race and as individuals. So often were they told openly and brutally that they were no good, that they were nothing, that they came to accept this negative image. "What can we do?" one hears an Indian say. "We are just Indians." Or, "How can we talk of equality? We will always be Indians no matter what we do. The government can't just suddenly rule that we are equal and make it a fact. Will the person who hated us yesterday because we are Indian love us tomorrow because the government says he should?"

Young Indians who went off to residential schools were obviously at a disadvantage. The missionary teachers soon made them aware of it if they didn't know it when they came. It doesn't take many times being called "an ungrateful little savage" to impress your difference upon you. And those who went into the white man's schools to be integrated found their little white friends brought their homes to the classroom: "My father says all Indians are drunks; my mother says Indians are dirty and I can't play with you." Indians who went to the cities to try to make their way found themselves isolated, pointed out, penalized for being Indian. Small wonder many Indians sought to hide their Indianness. They had lost their pride. They had overlooked the one thing they had that no white man had or has or can have—Indianness.

Today the trend is the other way. Young Indians are proud of their heritage and are learning more about it. During and after World War II many of our people crossed the colour line. It was a status thing to do. They had lived in a white world; they had fought as well as the white soldier. They were accepted for the time being, at least. Many married across the colour line. Now social pressure swings the other way with Indians, and is against marrying into white society.

Of course no one can deny there still are many negative factors relating, if not to actual Indian identity, then to the popular image of our identity. Indians are sensitive. We know that we may be turned away from the odd hotel because of our colour. We know that available suites at good highrise locations suddenly are taken when we show up. We are careful about the kind of restaurant we go into. But we also know that more and more Indians are suddenly standing straighter, walking with a firmer step and finding a new pride in being Indian.

The political aspect of our identity causes misunderstanding. In a meeting with the National Indian Brotherhood, Prime Minister Trudeau seemed concerned that a possible growth of separatism might exist among Indians. It is necessary to emphasize that the question of establishing a positive Indian identity does not mean political separatism—not yet, at least, not if the white man will agree to be reasonable—nor does it mean a desire to return to the days of yesteryear. The fact remains, however, that most Indians firmly believe their identity is tied up with treaty and aboriginal rights. Many Indians believe that until such rights are honoured there can be no Indian identity to take its place with the other cultural identities of Canada.

Our identity, who we are; this is a basic question that must be settled if we are to progress. A native person in Canada cannot describe himself without basically talking about himself as a Canadian. Being Canadian is implied and understood. To an Indian, being Indian in Canada simultaneously and automatically means being Canadian. The German Canadian has a homeland called Germany; the Ukrainian has a homeland;

even the French Canadian, although he may have ancestors going back three hundred years in Canadian history, has a homeland called France. The Indian's homeland is called Canada.

The challenge to Indians today is to redefine that identity in contemporary terminology. The challenge to the non-Indian society is to accept such an updated definition.

If I were to accept the bothersome term *Indian problem*, I would have to accept it in light of the fact that our most basic problem is gaining respect, respect on an individual basis that would make possible acceptance for us as an ethnic group. Before this is possible, the dignity, confidence and pride of the Indian people must be restored. No genuine Indian participation in the white world can be expected until the Indian is accepted by himself and by the non-Indian as an Indian person, with an Indian identity.

As long as Indian people are expected to become what they are not—white men—there does not and there will not exist a basis upon which they can participate in Canadian society.

Before we can demand acceptance by the white man, we must earn his respect. Before we can take our place in a larger society, we must regain our own confidence and self-respect. To do this we must be allowed to rebuild our own social institutions, torn down by their white counterparts. We must rebuild our structures of social and political leadership, demoralized and undermined for a hundred years by the Department of Indian Affairs; we must restore our family unit, shaken and shattered by the residential school system; we must rebuild communications between the younger and older generations of our people. We must recognize that the negative images of Indianness are false; the Canadian government must recognize that assimilation, no matter what they call it, will never work. Both Indian and non-Indian must realize that there is a valid, lasting Indian identity.

We are not interested, therefore, in the government's newest definition of who and what an Indian is, or must be. We have ceased to allow our identity to be a paperwork problem for members of the Department of Indian Affairs. Our people are now in the process of discovering what they are in a positive sense; Canadian society must accept us in a positive way before there can be an identification of common purpose and before true citizenship can develop. It is only when men are able to accept their differences as well as their similarities and still relate to each other with respect and dignity that a healthy society exists.

"As Long as the Rivers Run . . ."

With Forked Tongue

Everyone who has watched a late late movie on television sooner or later has found himself half-sleeping through one of the old-time westerns. Inevitably, at some point in the thriller a beaten travesty of Indian leadership draws his blanket around his shoulders and solemnly intones, "White man speaks with forked tongue." Even Indians laugh at a cliché like that, but their laughter is a little strained; the truth the phrase still tells, still rankles.

Our people believe very little the white man says, even today, because the white man continues to speak with forked tongue. Individual white men may not have to lie; they may, like the minister for Indian Affairs, his deputy minister, even our prime minister, be pedantically consistent in their own public statements about Indian policy. But when the position they have taken is a complete denial of promises the Canadian government once made to us and has always upheld (though never fulfilled), then their position, their statements represent an entire society's lie—the betrayal of the Indian people.

Our people no longer believe. It is that simple and it is that sad. The Canadian government can promise involvement, consultation, progressive human and economic development programmes. We will no longer believe them. The Canadian government can guarantee the most attractive system of education. We do not believe them. They can tell us their beautiful plans for the development of local self-government. We will shrug our disbelief. The government can create a hundred national Indian advisory councils to advise us about our problems. We will not listen to them. We will not believe what they say. The federal bureaucrats can meet with us one thousand times a year, but we will suspect

23

their motives. We will know they have nothing new to say. We will know they speak with forked tongue.

After generations of endless frustration with the Canadian government, our people are tired and impatient. *Before* the Canadian government tries to feed us hypocritical policy statements, more empty promises, more forked tonguistics, our people want, our people, the Indians, demand just settlement of all our treaty and aboriginal rights. Fulfillment of Indian rights by the queen's government must come before there can be any further cooperation between the Indians and the government. We demand nothing more. We expect nothing less.

Yes, the prime minister roused our hopes with his talk of a compassionate and just society. Then his minister for Indian Affairs told us our problems would vanish if we would become nice, manageable white men like all other Canadians. Just recently, the prime minister himself flicked the other fork of his tongue. In a speech in Vancouver, Mr. Trudeau said, "The federal government is not prepared to guarantee the aboriginal rights of Canada's Indians." Mr. Trudeau said, "It is inconceivable that one section of a society should have a treaty with another section of a society. The Indians should become Canadians as have all other Canadians."

Have other Canadians been led to this citizenship over a path of broken promises and dishonoured treaties?

To the Indians of Canada, the treaties represent an Indian Magna Carta. The treaties are important to us, because we entered into these negotiations with faith, with hope for a better life with honour. We have survived for over a century on little but that hope. Did the white man enter into them with something less in mind? Or have the heirs of the men who signed in honour somehow disavowed the obligation passed down to them? The Indians entered into the treaty negotiations as honourable men who came to deal as equals with the queen's representatives. Our leaders of that time thought they were dealing with an equally honourable people. Our leaders pledged themselves, their people and their heirs to honour what was done then.

Our leaders mistakenly thought they were dealing with an honourable people who would do no less than the Indians were doing—bind themselves, bind their people and bind their heirs to honourable contracts.

Our people talked with the government representatives, not as beggars pleading for handouts, but as men with something to offer in return for rights they expected. To our people, this was the beginning of a contractual relationship whereby the representatives of the queen would have lasting responsibilities to the Indian people in return for the valuable lands that were ceded to them.

The treaties were the way in which the white people legitimized in the eyes of the world their presence in our country. It was an attempt to settle the terms of occupancy on a just basis, legally and morally to extinguish the legitimate claims of our people to title to the land in our country. There never has been any doubt in the minds of our people that the land in Canada belonged to them. Nor can there have been any doubt in the mind of the government or in the minds of the white people about who owned the land, for it was upon the basis of white recognition of Indian rights that the treaties were negotiated. Otherwise, there could have been nothing to negotiate, no need for treaties. In the language of the Cree Indians, the Indian reserves are known as *the land that we kept for ourselves* or *the land that we did not give to the government.* In our language, *skun-gun.*

When one party to an agreement continually, ruthlessly breaks that agreement whenever it suits his purpose, the other partner cannot forever be expected to believe protestations of faith that accompany the next peace offering. In our society, a man who did not keep his part of a fair bargain, a man who used tricks and shady deals to wriggle out of commitments, a man who continually spoke with a forked tongue became known as a crook. Indians do not deal with cheats.

Mr. Chrétien says, "Get rid of the *Indian Act.* Treat Indians as any other Canadians." Mr. Trudeau says, "Forget the treaties. Let Indians become Canadians." This is the Just Society? To the Indian people, there can be no justice, no just society, until their rights are restored. Nor can there be any faith in Mr. Trudeau, Mr. Chrétien, the government, in white society until our rights are protected by lasting, equitable legislation.

As far as we are concerned our treaty rights represent a sacred, honourable agreement between ourselves and the Canadian government that cannot be unilaterally abrogated by the government at the whim of one of its leaders unless that government is prepared to give us back title to our country.

Our rights are too valuable to surrender to gallic or any other kind of rhetoric, too valuable to be sold for pieces of gold. Words change; the value of money fluctuates, may even disappear; our land will not disappear.

We cannot give up our rights without destroying ourselves as people. If our rights are meaningless, if it is inconceivable that our society have treaties with the white society even though those treaties were signed by honourable men on both sides, in good faith, long before the present government decided to tear them up as worthless scraps of paper, then we as a people are meaningless. We cannot and will not accept this. We know that as long as we fight for our rights we will survive. If we surrender, we die.

Currently, this lack of faith in our government, this feeling that our government speaks with a forked tongue is called a credibility gap. The credibility gap between the white society and Indian, between our government and our people must be closed. Our lack of faith in the federal government has far-reaching implications. As long as our rights are not honoured, and as long as the government continues to make it clear it has no intention of honouring them, then we must continue to be apprehensive about new plans such as the Chrétien policy to abolish the *Indian Act* and to do away with the Indian Affairs branch of the government. We will be fearful of any attempt by the federal government to turn over to provincial governments responsibility for Indian Affairs. We will be certain that the federal government is merely attempting to abandon its responsibilities. Provincial governments have no obligations to fulfill our treaties. They never signed treaties with the Indians. We could not expect them to be concerned with treaty rights. In our eyes, this new government policy merely represents a disguised move to abrogate all our treaty rights. This is our government speaking once again with forked tongue.

Until such time as the federal government accepts and protects our rights with abiding legislation, we will oppose and refuse to participate in any federal-provincial schemes that affect our rights.

Only fools believe even the most righteous assurances from those who consistently have refused to honour previous commitments, and only fools go on accepting forever further promises from such people. What are we to think when we are told the new government policy will abolish the Indian Affairs office within five years and then we learn of a letter signed by the deputy minister delivered to all employees in the department telling them not to be concerned about losing their jobs, advising them that a special task force has been set up to make certain they will not lose their civil service positions? What are we to think when the minister tells us we aren't supposed to be Indians any more, just Canadians like other Canadians, and then we learn of a letter making the rounds of the Indian Affairs offices advising that Indian "experts" will always be needed? What for? There are not supposed to be any more Indians.

The departmental letter goes on to explain that Indian experts or, at least, civil servants with "expert experience" will be needed in other ministries which will be taking over the problems of Indians—Health and Welfare, the Department of Economic Development—most departments, in fact. The letter advises that provincial governments will have places for many of them when those governments take over many of the duties of the department.

How much faith should we be expected to put in a policy which is born and delivered of forked tongue? How much faith should we be expected to put in a policy which merely proliferates the offices dealing in red tape and red Indians? Should we be expected to dance on the dirt floors of our cabins because we will now have some twenty more ministries with which to deal, when we are already strangling in red tape, about the only commodity freely dispensed by the one? Should we don buckskins and feathers to celebrate the arrival of the same old faces and the same old ideas at new and even less approachable desks?

By and large, the articles of all written treaties between the Indians of Canada and the government of Canada must be considered misleading because they omitted substantial portions of what was promised verbally to the Indian. Additionally, they carry key phrases that are not precise, or they state that certain things were ceded that, in actual fact, were never considered or granted by the Indians who signed the treaties. Nevertheless, the government, although not willing even to begin to honour its side of the partnership, holds Indians to the strictest letter of the treaties. According to government interpretation, the following outline represents the sum total of its commitment to the Indians involved in one particular, but typical treaty.

Under Treaty Six, the Indians involved (the Plain and Wood Cree tribes in Saskatchewan and Alberta) surrendered land comprising an approximate area of 121,000 square miles. Concerning land, written reports of the treaty make the following commitment: "And Her Majesty, the Queen, hereby agrees and undertakes to lay aside reserves for farming lands, due respect being had to lands at present cultivated by the said Indians, and other reserves for the benefit of the said Indians, to be administered and dealt with for them by Her Majesty's Government of the Dominion of Canada; provided all such reserves shall not exceed in all one square mile for each family of five or in that proportion for larger or smaller families.... The Chief Superintendent of Indian Affairs shall depute and send a suitable person to determine and set apart the reserves for each band, after consulting with the Indians thereof as to the locality which may be found to be most suitable for them."

In the field of education, Treaty Six states: "Her Majesty agrees to maintain schools for instruction in such reserves hereby made as to Her Government of the Dominion of Canada may deem advisable, whenever the Indians of the reserve shall desire it."

The government also promised under treaty to give the Indians "the right to pursue their avocations of hunting and fishing throughout the tract surrendered as hereintofor described, subject to such regulations as may from time to time be made by Her Government of Her Dominion of Canada." The formal statement on aboriginal rights also outlines hunting restrictions in areas of settlement, mining or lumbering.

Surprisingly, many non-Indian people believe that the Indians receive all the money they need from the government throughout the year. In the Prairie provinces, the Indians were promised that the government would "pay to each Indian person the sum of $5.00 per head yearly."

In order to assist the Indians to make a beginning in farming, the government made the following commitment: "four hoes for every family actually cultivating; also, two spades per family aforesaid; one plough for every three families as aforesaid; one harrow for every three families as aforesaid; two scythes and one whetstone, and two hay forks and two reaping hooks, for every family aforesaid and also two axes; and also one crosscut saw, one hand-saw, one pit-saw, the necessary files, one grindstone and one auger for each band; and also for each chief for the use of his band, one chest of ordinary carpenter's tools; also, for each band, enough of wheat, barley, potatoes and oats to plant the land actually broken up for cultivation by such band; also for each band four oxen, one bull and six cows; also, one boar and two sows and one hand-mill when any band shall raise sufficient grain therefor."

Recognition of leadership was given: chiefs were to be paid an "annual salary of twenty-five dollars per annum and each subordinate officer, not exceeding four for each band, shall receive fifteen dollars per annum … shall receive once every three years a suitable suit of clothing and each chief shall receive in recognition of the closing of the treaty a suitable flag and medal and also as soon as convenient, one horse, harness and wagon."

The promise of medical care was contained in the following phrase: "A medicine chest shall be kept at the house of each Indian agent for the use and benefit of the Indians at the directions of such agent."

Under Treaty Six, welfare or social assistance was promised under the phrase, "In the event hereafter of the Indians comprised within this treaty being overtaken by any pestilence or by a general famine, the Queen, on being satisfied and certified thereof by Her Indian agent or agents will grant to the Indians assistance of such character and to such extent as Her Chief Superintendent of Indian Affairs [the minister] shall deem necessary and sufficient to relieve the Indians from the calamity that shall have befallen them."

These pledges are typical, if not all-inclusive, of the promises that were made to the Indians by the government, although the cautionary phrase, "Her Majesty reserves the right to deal with...," appearing commonly throughout the treaty, would have alerted a more sophisticated people to possible loopholes and pitfalls. There are many other aspects of the written treaties that are questionable. Generally, the treaties are outstanding for what they *do not* say rather than what they do say.

In spite of their admissions and omissions the treaties are doubly significant and important because they represent or imply principles that are intrinsically part of the concept of justice and respect for other men's property. They have a symbolic importance to Indians that cannot be ignored.

Many people, including the prime minister, have suggested that treaties are problems of yesteryear. They suggest that Indian treaties are irrelevant to life in the twentieth century and that to consider them important now is to look at life backwards, that we should forget the past and the treaties and look only toward the future. This position was put forward by Mr. Chrétien at the national consultation meetings (between the government and representatives of all Canada's Indians) held in Ottawa April 28–May 2, 1969. It is difficult to understand how this government or any government could adopt such a position. For the Trudeau government, preoccupied as it has been with language rights, the Canadian constitution, the criminal code and the concept of human rights, it becomes doubly a paradox.

If this government really wants to insist that the question of treaties is a problem of yesteryear then, to be consistent, the government must admit that it is itself a backward-looking government. It admits to a preoccupation with problems dating back to 1867 in the case of the constitution, back much farther in its concerns with language rights, human rights and the criminal code. Rather than denigrating our viewpoint as backward and thereby delaying solutions to the many pressing problems faced by Indians, the time has come for the government to recognize that the question of Indian rights must be settled immediately. Only when this is accomplished can the problems of hunger, of joblessness, of lack of education and opportunity be faced. If the government would even indicate a willingness to try to live up to its obligations, many problems would vanish.

There have been sporadic indications of the growth of a red power faction in Canada, paralleling to a degree the rise of black power in the United States. Some individual Indians and some Indian organizations have suggested that more adroit use of political power or the even uglier use of physical strength (both to be achieved through more effective organization and evidenced by protest demonstrations) would be more effective than continued efforts to talk to a government which refuses to listen. Students of Indian affairs have noted that one finds many indications among Indians of an appreciation of the principle of sovereignty, and note the recurrence of such phraseology as "We are sovereign nations." Some government officials have even suggested that financial assistance to native organizations would foster separatism among the Indian people in Canada.

People who think this adds up to leanings toward separatism among Indians do not know and have not even begun to understand the basic concerns of our people. However, as long as the government persists in denying to our people the legislation necessary for the protection of our rights, our people must be expected to look for alternatives. Who can say at what point such alternatives may become viable?

Once our rights are guaranteed, there will be less need for our people to emphasize their sovereignty. The question of Indian rights is the paramount question for all Indian people from the vantage point of the past, the present and the future.

While we find much to quarrel with in the treaties as they were signed, they are, we contend, important, not so much for their content as for the principles they imply in their very existence.

The Manitoba Indian Brotherhood, under its progressive and capable president, David Courchene, made the following observations about the treaties during their regional consultation meetings in December 1968.

"From reading these treaties it is apparent that:

1. The officials representing the Government full well knew the value of the land requested to be ceded to the Crown;
2. ... they were aware that the Indian was not able to communicate with them;
3. ... the Indian had no counsel;
4. ... the Indian was impressed by the pomp and ceremony and the authority of the officials;
5. ... they [the officials] were dealing with uneducated people;
6. ... the respect and ceremony with which the officials were dealing with the Indians lulled the Indians into a passive mood;
7. ... a father image was being advanced by the authorities;
8. ... the Indians, although it is alleged were explained the terms of the Treaties, really did not know or understand fully the meaning and implications;
9. ... the alleged consideration that was being advanced by the Government to the Indians in exchange for the ceded land was not totally appreciated by the Indians, nor could they understand the concept of binding their heirs and executors, administrators and assigns to these documents;
10. ... forever and a day it will be obvious to all who read the said Treaties and the history of their making, that the officials of Her Majesty the Queen committed a legal fraud in a very sophisticated manner upon unsophisticated, unsuspecting, illiterate, uninformed natives."

Manitoba's Indians, taking for the first time a hard look at the past, said, "These treaties must be renegotiated." Their study of the past pointed the way to the future.

We can brook no argument that the treaties are not relevant to the present. They are related in a very direct way to the hunting, trapping and fishing rights of our people because, even today, a large portion of the Indian people still depend upon these rights for their livelihood. Our rights are today's problem, for upon them the education of our people rests. Access to medical services, upon which our people depend, proportionately, more than any other Canadians for their health and well-being, is entirely at the pleasure of the government. Our rights are even more relevant today when one considers the need for land and the need for future economic development.

The future of the Indian in Canada lies in the area of education, proper medical services, land and economic development. There is no future for our people if the government does not respect and protect our rights.

The Indians of Alberta made their position clear to the government when they demanded that legislation be passed to protect:

1. hunting, trapping and fishing rights,
2. the right of education,
3. the right of full and free medical services,
4. the right of land,

and to encourage

5. economic development on reserves.

"The terms of the treaties," insisted the Manitoba Indian Brotherhood, "must be extended and interpreted in light of present social and economic standards. To renegotiate the treaties does not necessarily mean to rewrite the treaties, nor does it mean to repudiate the treaties."

It was recognized at the Manitoba meeting that the importance of the treaties lies in the recognition and acceptance of the true spirit of the treaties rather than studied adherence to archaic phraseology.

The brotherhood noted: "A promise by the Government and a carrying out of that promise to give economic and financial assistance to the Indian so that he may better be able to advance his economic position in the community, would be a carrying out of one of the terms of the treaties. A promise and a carrying out of that promise by the Government that every child will have the right to a full education with all facilities made available to him for that purpose, is a carrying out of one of the terms of the treaties. A guarantee that every Indian will have full and adequate and immediate medical treatment as and when required, is a carrying out of one of the terms of those treaties.

"To renegotiate those treaties means to reach agreement, to carry out the full meaning and intent of the promises given by the representatives of the Queen, as interpreted, and as understood by the Indians. To successfully renegotiate those treaties is to bring about a legal commitment by the Government that the true intent and tenure of those treaties will be carried out."

The Indian people cannot be blamed for feeling that not until the sun ceases to shine, the rivers cease to flow and the grasses to grow or, wonder of wonders, the government decides to honour its treaties, will the white man cease to speak with forked tongue.

The
Great Swindle

Precedent for Betrayal

The way it stands now, the much laughed-at American Indians who sold all of Manhattan Island for twenty-four dollars' worth of beads and trinkets got a better deal than Canadian Indians. The white man has never conducted such a clearly defined exchange with our people. There are precedents for the present government's betrayal; the white man took what we gave him, and more, but we never received payment. It was planned that way.

The truth of the matter is that Canadian Indians simply got swindled. Our forefathers got taken by slick-talking, fork-tongued cheats. It wasn't their fault. Our forefathers, with possibly a few cynical exceptions, never understood the white man. They had fought battles, known victory and defeat, but treachery was new to them. They were accustomed to trusting another man's word, even an enemy's.

The Indian leaders who signed our treaties with the representatives of the government of Canada came to the signatory negotiations and meetings with honourable intent and laudable purpose. Their gravest mistake was to give the white man the benefit of the doubt and attribute to him the same high principles. He didn't have them. He, the white man, talked one way and wrote another.

Not only was much of what was written in the treaties written without the full understanding of the Indians involved; much more which the Indian expected to be in the treaties never was written. Preceding the writing of the treaties, the white man and the Indian talked and what the white man said was reassuring. His promises and reassurances without doubt helped to convince the Indian leaders they could and should sign the treaties in good conscience. They had no way of knowing their opposites would not put in writing what they had put in words.

How do we know that this happened? By word of mouth from Indian father to son, of course, but the official reports of the commissioners for the treaties provide more interesting clues.

In the "Report of Commissioners for Treaty No. 8," Commissioner David Laird stated: "There was expressed at every point the fear that the making of the treaty would be followed by the curtailment of hunting and fishing privileges, and many were impressed with the notion that the treaty would lead to taxation and enforced military service."

He wrote, "We promised that supplies of medicine would be put in the charge of persons selected by the Government at different points, and would be distributed free to those of the Indians who might require them."

The report says: "Our chief difficulty was the apprehension that the hunting and fishing privileges were to be curtailed. The provision in the treaty under which ammunition and twine is to be furnished went far in the direction of quieting the fears of the Indians, for they admitted that it would be unreasonable to furnish the means of hunting and fishing if laws were to be enacted which would make hunting and fishing so restricted as to render it impossible to make a livelihood by such pursuits. But over and above the provision, we had to solemnly assure them that only such laws as to hunting and fishing as were in the interests of the Indians and were found necessary in order to protect the fish and fur-bearing animals would be made, and that they would be as free to hunt and fish after the treaty as they would be if they never entered into it."

This written report is not recognized as a commitment of any nature by the government. The articles of Treaty Eight, which are recognized as the commitment of the government, are as follows: "And Her Majesty the Queen hereby agrees with the said Indians that they shall have the right to pursue their usual vocations of hunting, trapping and fishing throughout the tract surrendered as heretofore described, subject to such regulations as may from time to time be made by the Government of the country, acting under the authority of Her Majesty, and saving and excepting such tracts as may be required or taken up from time to time for settlement, mining, lumbering, trading or other purposes."

So we see that, in spite of obvious verbal assurances that there would be no restrictions on the hunting, trapping and fishing rights of the people, provisions were made under the articles of the treaty to allow for legislation to be enacted without the knowledge of the Indians and without concern for the preservation of the species but for any purpose which might occur to the government. It was just such a situation that took the right of the Indian to kill ducks for food recently.

Two of the most controversial items resulting from the manner in which the treaties were written remain the mineral rights and the headland-to-headland issues.

Most treaties have within them the following phrase: "The said Indians do hereby cede, release, surrender and yield up to the Government of the Dominion of Canada, for Her Majesty the Queen and Her successors for ever, all their rights, titles and privileges whatsoever, to the lands. . . ." As far as the Indian signatories were concerned, and certainly in line with Indian thinking today, the treaties were not intended to take away Indian mineral rights. The treaties, as our people understood them, meant the surrender of surface rights only so that the land could be shared with other peoples, without jeopardy to Indian claims to what lay under the surface.

Many of the reserves that were taken by the Indians were situated around or in close proximity to lakes and rivers. The underlying purpose in so locating the reserves was to give the people access to one of their traditional means of livelihood—fishing. Therefore, when the land was taken for a reserve, the headland-to-headland concept was adopted. This means that parts of the waters, lakes or rivers were incorporated into the reserves so that the Indians there could continue to fish and hunt water fowl unmolested. The government has yet to acknowledge ownership by the Indians of those portions of land under water.

Obviously, both in the case of mineral rights and in the sub-surface water rights, vast amounts of money could be involved. Opportunities for Indians to advance their own economic development could be at stake.

Treaty Eight in many ways exemplifies the manner in which the government representatives worked legally to swindle our people. They promised everything. They wrote bloody little.

The report of the commissioners states: "We promised that supplies of medicines would be put in the charge of persons selected by the Government at different points, and would be distributed free to those of the Indians who might require them. . . . We assured them . . . that the Government would always be ready to avail itself of any opportunity of affording medical service just as it provided that the physician attached to the Commission should give free attendance to all Indians whom he might find in need of treatment as he passed through the country." Yet the main articles of the treaty do not in any way refer to medical services or rights to free medical attention.

The commissioner admits on record that the Indians were assured of medicine and medical treatment. The Indians expected this to be in the treaty. They were not told it was not there. Legally, the commitment is not there in the treaty. Legally, the white man clearly won that round. Ethically, it is damned comforting to be Indian.

In relation to education the government representatives made the following observation: "They seemed desirous of securing educational advantages for their children, but stipulated that in the matter of schools there should be no interference with their religious beliefs.... As to education, the Indians were assured that there was no need of any special stipulation, as it was the policy of the Government to provide in every part of the country, as far as circumstances would permit, for the education of Indian children, and that the law, which was as strong as a treaty, provided for non-interference with the religion of the Indians in schools maintained or assisted by the Government."

The main article of the treaty simply states: "Further, Her Majesty agrees to pay the salaries of such teachers to instruct the children of said Indians as to her Majesty's Government of Canada may seem advisable."

The Indian people clearly understood that free education would be provided. This they were promised verbally—if the commissioners' report can be taken at face value. Yet the written guarantee in the treaty stipulated no such thing. Deceived again by the noble white man.

Much research must be done to trace and pin down all such examples of moral lapse. Much work must be done to alleviate the immoral situation created by such double-dealing. However, inadequate and highly questionable as the treaties are, they are important, for they symbolize the commitment of the government to our people.

Indians wryly joke that a native can't even get sick without written permission of the Indian agent. It isn't quite that bad, but the reality is not far from the jest.

The responsibility for discharging the provisions of the Indian treaties fell entirely to the dominion government by subsection 24 and section 91 of the British North America Act of 1867, which gave the Parliament of Canada the exclusive power to deal with "Indians and lands reserved for Indians." To deal with the administrators of the reserves provided for in the treaties and the question of the status of Indians, the federal government passed legislation in 1868 under which reserves were placed in the sphere of the Department of the Secretary of State. This was followed in 1869 by legislation which dealt to a greater extent with the legal rights of Indians. Both those acts were then consolidated by Parliament in 1880. The provisions of the 1880 act were substantially the same as those of the present-day *Indian Act*, with the only major revision occurring in 1951.

The *Indian Act* was passed with the intention of implementing the terms of the treaties and of establishing the status of Indians. It was made the main body of law from which the legal rights of Indians flow. This was one of the first major steps taken by the government of Canada to weaken the treaties signed with our people, for now it is from the *Indian Act* that the legal position of the Indian primarily stems, rather than from the treaties themselves. This piece of legislation that was supposed to implement the terms of the treaties was surely written by people who understood or cared very little about protecting human rights but who were thoroughly concerned and familiar with concepts and laws characteristic of colonial powers.

The *Indian Act*, instead of implementing the treaties and offering much-needed protection to Indian rights, subjugated to colonial rule the very people whose rights it was supposed to protect.

For example, all lands on the reserves are held by the queen for the use and benefit of the Indian bands for whom the reserves were set apart. Accordingly, section 18 of the act gives the minister responsible a discretionary power to authorize the use of reserve land for schools, hospitals and various other projects which the minister may desire to initiate once the consent of the band has been obtained. An individual Indian living on the reserve can't work up much interest in improving or even maintaining his home because he cannot by law even acquire title to the land on which he resides. If he makes improvements to the land, he does so at the risk of later being removed from it by the minister or one of his agents without receiving one iota of compensation for the improvements.

Local government of the reserve lies largely in the hands of the Department of Indian Affairs and Northern Development. Under section 72 of the *Indian Act*, the governor in council is invested with discretionary power to make regulations for such matters as medical treatment, hospitalization and health services on the reserves. In addition, he may provide for the inspection of dwellings and make regulations concerning sanitary conditions in both public and private premises.

Section 73 of the act allows the minister, when he deems it necessary for the good government of the reserve, to declare that a band council may be elected by all persons of twenty-one years of age on the reserve. The council consists of one chief and one councillor for every hundred members of the band provided that there shall never be more than twelve nor less than two councillors. Under section 80 the band council is authorized to make bylaws for such matters as the health of band members, regulation of reserve traffic, construction and maintenance of roads, ditches and fences and the use of all public facilities. This, of course, is power of a sort, self-government of a sort, except that any by-laws enacted by the band may be disallowed by the minister or his agent and must not contravene any regulations made under the *Indian Act*.

The finances of the reserves are almost exclusively under the control of the Department of Indian Affairs acting through the powers of the minister. Both the capital and revenue monies of the band are held by the government in a consolidated revenue fund. (Capital monies are defined as those derived primarily from the sale of surrendered lands or capital assets while revenue monies are obtained primarily from the sale of the jointly-owned produce of the band.) Together these monies constitute the entire band fund, comprising all financial assets of the band. Under section 64 the minister may, with the consent of the band council, direct the expenditure of these monies for various public works and/or welfare projects. The band council, however, is powerless to make such expenditures without the consent of the minister.

Except possibly for the slight ameliorating effect of sections 86–89, the *Indian Act*, that piece of colonial legislation, enslaved and bound the Indian to a life under a tyranny often as cruel and harsh as that of any totalitarian state. The only recourse allowed victims of the act is enfranchisement, whereby the Indian is expected to deny his birthright, declare himself no longer an Indian and leave the reserve, divesting himself of all his interest in his land and people. This course of action is one that any human being would hesitate to take. To the Indian it means that he must leave his home, the community of his family, to which neither he nor his wife nor his children may ever return. All this to enter a society which he generally finds prejudiced against him.

Section 87 of the *Indian Act* reads: "Subject to the terms of any treaty and any other Act of the Parliament of Canada, all laws of general application from time to time in force in any province are applicable to and in respect of Indians in the province, except to the extent that such laws are inconsistent with this Act or any order, rule, regulation or by-law made thereunder, and except to the extent that such laws make provision for any matter for which provision is made by or under this Act."

Section 87 ostensibly was inserted into the *Indian Act* to protect the rights of our people from encroachment by provincial laws. The weakness of the section lies in the fact that it did not and does not apply to laws enacted by the Parliament of Canada.

In the Canadian legal system, the application of provincial statutes to Indians and Indian reserves has been determined largely through cases arising from attempts by provincial authorities to bring Indians within the operation of provincial game laws. Under our treaties, we generally were guaranteed the right to hunt and fish over all the lands ceded to the crown except where such lands were taken up for settlement. Under cases tried in provincial courts, decisions have been reached whereby the native person was allowed to hunt for food on all unoccupied crown lands in any season, but was restricted by the game laws of the province as to the methods he might use. This ruling prevailed despite the fact that the Indian could not be forced by the province to purchase hunting licences or observe other provincial game regulations.

Practically, this interpretation meant that we would lose our right to hunt, in spite of our treaties, whenever any supposed important conservation principle was incorporated into a provincial statute.

The final blow to our cherished and necessary hunting rights was delivered by the Supreme Court of Canada, in one of the strangest rulings in court history, when an Indian in the Northwest Territories was convicted of killing a wild duck for food, contrary to the regulations made by the federal government under section 12 of the Migratory Birds Convention Act. This decision stated that our treaty rights were subject to the laws of the Parliament of Canada and, as such, any federal legislation affecting our rights would supersede the rights we are entitled to under the treaties.

The court itself admitted that in handing down such a ruling it was abrogating the treaties. Where or when before has a nation's highest court so blithely and without compassion declared its own government to be dishonouring its sacred commitments?

Time and time again, in the very department that was set up to protect our rights, decisions have been made that openly flaunt the treaties.

On the question of our right to education, the Department of Indian Affairs holds the policy that education is a privilege—not a right. Our treaties expressly say otherwise. As for medical and health services, the Department of National Health and Welfare holds the policy that medical health services are provided to Indians on the basis of need and indigency—not on the basis of treaty rights. Even many Indian people are unaware that their rights have been so ruthlessly trampled. As far as our people are concerned, medicare comes under treaty rights. Medicare should be paid for by the government. At a recent meeting on one of our reserves, representatives of the Department of National Health and Welfare told Indians there that medicare would be handled on the same basis as medical services had been before, that is, as treaty rights. These representatives were either ignorant or lying. The issues of who would pay for medicare premiums and what services medicare would provide were never explained and the people were left uninformed—worse, misinformed. From such situations come unnecessary misunderstandings, and no rationalizations will convince our people that this was not another case of forked tongue.

Together, actions of the government and decisions of the courts of Canada have demoted the Indian treaties to the status of mere ancient promises or agreements between the Indians and the dominion, promises which may be forgotten or abrogated at any time by the federal government.

However, the doors are not closed. The treaty situation has many ramifications. The position taken by the Indians of Canada at the national consultation meetings of April 28–May 2, 1969, was that no discussion would take place on changes in the *Indian Act* until our rights were secured and protected by the federal government. The response of Minister of Indian Affairs Jean Chrétien, that the federal government intended to honour the treaties, was something less than credible. His June announcement of a radical new federal Indian policy set in motion the government's plan finally and formally to repudiate the treaties. The new plan would abolish the *Indian Act* within five years and surrender federal jurisdiction to the provinces with no accompanying assurances that our rights will be honoured. It has widened the credibility gap and angered all native people as yet another attempt by the government to shuck off its responsibilities.

In spite of this giant step in the wrong direction, the federal government does have available a number of alternatives with which to meet the legitimate grievances of our people. It would be well advised at this time, in view of the premature policy announcement by Mr. Chrétien, to wait until the work of the Indian National Committee, chosen at the national consultation meetings, is finished. The committee plans to research and document the treaty rights of the Canadian Indian. Once this is completed, the Indians of Canada will be able to present to the government a petition of rights supported by documentation, for the purpose of having those rights protected by abiding legislation and/or inclusion into the Canadian constitution.

The work of the National Committee can in many ways be compared to the work of the B & B Commission as a prelude to the languages bill that Parliament recently passed. The basic rights of our people are no more negotiable than was the status of the French language.

Our need now, and an urgent task for the government of Canada, is the creation of lasting legislation for the protection of our rights. The mistake of 1868, whereby a government department was made responsible for the protection and implementation of our rights, must not be repeated.

Nothing less than new structures created in consultation with Indians and with the involvement of Indians will be acceptable. The new formula or structure must make provision for the protection of native rights but it must be subject to joint control of the government and the Indian people. We can no longer tolerate a monolithic big-brother or great-white-father arrangement. A new control structure might take the shape of a permanent commission or a crown corporation under Indian authority. Such a commission or corporation could be responsible for the vital land trusteeship and fulfill a watch-dog role over legislation that might conflict with rights granted under treaty.

With such constant consultation, the present role of the Department of Indian Affairs could be phased out as Mr. Chrétien has suggested, but only as development occurs at the reserve level. This means that attention would have to be concentrated upon many areas presently neglected by the department. Later, an accelerated pace of development could be carried out in conjunction with existing Indian organizations and local band councils. Each of the provincial organizations can play an important role in assuring and facilitating the implementation of urgently needed educational training and economic development on the reserves within their respective provinces.

Immediately and vitally needed is a claims commission, long promised and equally long stalled by several governments, for the settlement of many outstanding claims that Indians have, outside their basic rights. Such a commission would be concerned with claims of Indians in British Columbia, the territories and other areas of Canada where no treaties have been signed, as well as in those areas where treaty claims have been brushed aside. In many instances such claims will have to do with land that was illegally and/or unconscionably taken from Indians. Some such claims already have been placed before the courts of Canada. A claims commission should take over jurisdiction of all such cases. The claims commission, to have credibility, must be created and set up in close consultation with the Indian leaders of the country.

The Department of Indian Affairs has lost the confidence of our people. As protectors of our rights, their credibility is in a state of total bankruptcy. To regain the confidence of our people, the government of Canada must reinstate our treaties. Upon this foundation and upon this foundation only, the government of Canada still can embark on an honourable undertaking with the Indian peoples.

The Little
Red Schoolhouse

Gallons of White Paint

Indians sometimes think that if government authorities became convinced they could solve the Indian problem by purchasing gallons of white paint and painting all of us white, they would not hesitate to try. In fact, the government's education policy almost seems aimed in that direction. Indians recognize that education is one of the major tools that will help us strike off the shackles of poverty and, incidentally, the tyranny of government direction. But the white man apparently believes that education is a tool for the implementation of his design of assimilation.

Until these poles-apart goals of education can be made compatible, the full benefits that the institution has to offer our people will never be realized.

The government naïvely believes it can assimilate our people. Many authorities foolishly believe that genuine integration can be imposed upon the Indian people from the top, through means which can only be termed unscrupulous and devious. To the Indian mind, integration—or assimilation—has no more rightful place in government programming than would an attempt to integrate Roman Catholics and Jehovah's Witnesses. And about as much chance of succeeding.

The whole question of education has to be rethought in the light of the total needs of the Indian people. The obvious first step is the transfer of power from the people responsible for the administration of education to the people whose lives will be determined by it. No educational programme can be successful and, it follows, no society can be successful, where the people most directly concerned and affected have no voice whatever in their own education.

In the old days the Indian peoples had their own system of education.

Although the system was entirely informal and varied from tribe to tribe or location to location, it had one great factor going for it—it worked. The Indian method, entirely pragmatic, was designed to prepare the child for whatever way of life he was to lead—hunter, fisherman, warrior, chief, medicine man or wife and mother.

Children of each sex were trained to perform the various functions that would be expected of them once they assumed their eventual place in the social strata. Generally the band elders or wisemen, in conjunction with the parents, were responsible for the value orientation of the child. This education-to-a-purpose enabled the child gradually to become a functioning, contributing part of his society. Since all of the social institutions of his society were intact, he was able to become part of and relate to a stable social system. His identity was never a problem. His education had fitted him to his society; he knew who he was and how he related to the world and the people about him.

The arrival of the white man and the missionaries brought into the Indian world different values, different concepts of life that gravely disrupted the social institutions of the Indian. The missionaries, in particular, introduced two critically important institutions—religion and formal education. The introduction of these institutions to the Indian heralded a new era, drastically changing the old way of life. The missionaries promulgated a completely foreign culture with values which in many cases, generations later, still are foreign to the Indian.

It is unfair to judge the dismal record in Indian education without looking at the history of Canada's attempts formally to educate the Indian. The Canadian government inexplicably did not participate actively in an education programme for Indian children until the early 1950s and did not vigorously pursue that policy until the mid- or later fifties.

Prior to the 1950s the responsibility for educating Indian children fell into the hands of the missionaries. Much can be said about the inherent good intentions of these people, and it is true that without their efforts the educational level of our people might be even lower than it is today. Unfortunately, much more has to be said about the role the misguided missionaries played in the disruption of the Indians' way of life and their direct responsibility for the failure of Indians to achieve educational parity with non-Indian society.

The unvarnished truth is that the missionaries of all Christian sects regarded the Indians as savages, heathens or something even worse.

They made no attempt to understand Indian religious beliefs, virtually no attempt to appreciate Indian cultural values and paid little heed to Indian ways. The true purpose of the schools they established was to process good little Christian boys and girls—but only Christians of the sect operating the school. In those early church schools, academic knowledge occupied one of the back seats. Since the Indian was expected to live in isolation from the rest of society, obviously all the education he needed was a bit of reading, writing, figures and some notion of hygiene.

The employment of missionaries as the educational agent of the non-Indian society came about naturally enough. As white settlers encroached more and more onto Indian lands, the government employed multiple forces, the missionaries, the police, the Hudson's Bay Company and its own Indian agents, as salesmen for its own pacification programme. Because the missionaries had brought a message of a better life to the Indians, their reception had been open armed and their rapport with the Indians established early. They were interested primarily in a high conversion score. The government was interested in keeping the savages quiet. Their aims dovetailed, and the Indian was the pawn.

The first schools created by the missionaries were residential schools. This system was considered functional because the nomadic life of the Indian prevented his permanent establishment at one location. The residential school system allowed the family provider to roam the wilderness as hunter or trapper while, at the same time, his children were being educated at a residential school where they stayed ten months of the year, sometimes the year round.

In addition to turning out pious little Christians of their own sect, and there was fierce competition among the sects for bodies which might presumably be turned into souls, the schools served the purpose of keeping the parents under the influence of the church concerned. The church's educational function also assured it a more dominant role in formation of government policy, and the missionaries were expert at playing off the Indian against the civil servant. This uneasy government-church alliance continued until the 1950s. The government was happy to have the Indians domesticated without the expenditure necessary to handle the job itself. The churches obtained government money to keep the schools operating so they could continue their real work, the conversion of the Indian people. Between them, and with no question of any involvement of the Indians, the government and the churches charted for eighty years or more the future of the Indian people.

In plain words the system was lousy. The curriculum stank, and the teachers were misfits and second raters. Even in my own elementary school days, in grade eight I found myself taking over the class because my teacher, a misfit, has-been or never-was sent out by his superiors from Quebec to teach savages in a wilderness school because he had failed utterly in civilization, couldn't speak English well enough to make himself understood. Naturally, he knew no Cree. When we protested such inequities we were silenced as "ungrateful little savages who don't
√ appreciate what is being done for you."

Under the circumstances, any successes in education through the residential school system emerged as exceptions rather than the rule. The residential schools even failed in their first purpose—turning out good little Christians. They alienated the child from his own family; they alienated him from his own way of life without in any way preparing him for a different society; they alienated the child from his own religion and turned his head resolutely against the confusing substitute the missionaries offered. Worst of all, perhaps, the entire misconceived approach, the illogical (to the Indian children) disciplines enforced, the failure to relate the new education in any pragmatic way to their lives turned the child against education, prevented him from seeing or appreciating the benefits of a real education. For the Canadian Indian, the lack of educational opportunities prior to the mid-fifties marks those generations as a time of neglect which is still taking its toll.

In the mid-fifties the government finally awakened to its responsibilities toward Indian children. The transition from denominational schools to the joint schools devised by the federal government confused the Indian in many instances, but one factor remained constant. Before the direct governmental entry into native education the churches promulgated education programmes in isolation from the Indian people concerned. The government made no change in that respect and still pushes its programme without the involvement of the native peoples. Aims of the federally sponsored education differ, however. The obvious aim now is integration or, to be more precise, assimilation of the Indian.

The Hawthorn report observes: "As we have emphasized, the general aim of the federal government's present policy is based on the necessity
√ of integrating Indians into Canadian society. Education is considered the principal means for achieving this aim. The secondary aims are to provide Indians with a degree of economic and social welfare equivalent

to that of non-Indians and to provide them with the knowledge which they will need to live adequately within their own environment."

These objectives are further defined in a document entitled *The Administration of Indian Affairs*: "The educational system administered by the Indian Affairs Branch attempts to provide a complete educational programme for every Indian child according to individual needs, local circumstances and the wishes of the parents. Its objective is to assist the Indian people in bridging the socio-economic gap between the Indian and non-Indian in Canada, and to provide each child with the education and the training necessary for economic competence." Hence, the aim is to raise the educational standards of Indians to a level equivalent to that of the province in which they live, to prepare them for remunerative employment and, eventually, urban life.

School integration of Indians with non-Indians is seen as the primary means of attaining this long-term objective. Several texts are explicit on this point. The following excerpts cited in the Hawthorn report are typical:

> It is the policy of the department to educate Indian children wherever possible in association with other children, particularly where accommodation is available and practical in a provincial school system and provided the Indians approve.
>
> (*Observations on the Integration Program, Education Division*)

The last phrase—"provided the Indians approve"—may be allowed in theory but in practice, it hasn't worked that way. No one bothers to ask the Indians.

> Overall planning ... is based on the assumption that all Indian children should receive their education in association with other Canadian children.
>
> We believe that by having Indian children and other Canadian children grow up and play together in the same school yard, they will work together better in later life.
>
> (*New Directions in Indian Affairs*)

Obviously, beyond any question, the integration programme constitutes the central point of the federal government's policy in the field of Indian education.

Government plans for the future of Indian education display the same inherent weakness of government programmes of the past and present —they propose theoretical objectives as practical solutions to existing problems, a flaw fatal to any school system. However, the greatest weakness of government programming, both now and for the future, lies in the fact that there is no direct consultation with or involvement of our people. Can we be blamed for suspecting that the government's real policy is assimilation, thinly disguised under the more acceptable term, integration?

In its unseemly haste to ram its integration or assimilation policy down our throats, the government often fails to follow through on programmes. Indian children have been forced to attend local provincial schools before adequate arrangements have been completed to look after their interests. Local school boards piously open their schools for integration, ostensibly to offer Indian children greater opportunities. What they really want is the per capita school payment they earn from federal coffers by opening their doors to Indians. Their interest in the welfare and education of their new charges is usually minimal.

Curiously, integration seems to be a one-way street with the government. Always it is the Indian who must integrate into the white environment, never the other way around. Integration apparently can happen only in schools off the reserves. No thought is given to building facilities on the reserve, where feasible, so that integration might have a chance to work within an Indian environment. Perhaps if this were tried, there would be less assimilation and more integration in the programme.

Hawthorn, in his *Survey of the Contemporary Indians of Canada*, notes: "The government's policy on the preservation of Indian languages and cultural traditions, for example, is not clear. As a general rule they are not assigned much importance. This makes it difficult to distinguish between a policy of integration and a policy of assimilation, which allows the loss of the basic cultural values of the integrated ethnic group."

To appreciate the difficulty of implementing such a policy, one has to examine the bureaucratic system that has evolved. This is the sort of bureaucratic jungle into which a poor Indian could disappear for months, emerging, if ever, wrapped up in red tape like a mummy.

The Education Division of the Department of Indian Affairs encompasses seven school regions: the Maritimes, Quebec, Ontario, Manitoba, Saskatchewan, Alberta and British Columbia. Each region in turn is subdivided into a number of agencies. As the need for new agencies occurs, new districts are created, each comprising two, three or more agencies. This bureaucratic structure is itself superimposed on the general bureaucratic structure of the Department of Indian Affairs and Northern Development. A man could spend his lifetime burrowing through division desks just looking for an official to complain to about the difficulty of finding that particular official.

The regional school superintendent works under the regional director of Indian Affairs. Where a district office exists, a district school superintendent follows the position of the regional office. Where there are no district offices, the regional superintendent is followed by the agency school superintendent or supervising principal. The regional school superintendent is responsible for interpreting the policies of the Department of Indian Affairs concerning Indian education. He also prepares projections of expanding needs and is responsible for the administration of the entire school system. The district superintendent has three duties: organizing classes, administering individual schools and supervising schools. Are you still with me, or were you left behind with the Indians? Communications in a bureaucratic structure normally take place between superior and immediate subordinates all the way down the chain of authority, assuming, of course, they can figure out just who the superiors and subordinates are.

The Hawthorn report comments: "Thus the district school superintendent and the agency supervising principal are both liable to consult the agency superintendent on a similar problem or at least problems of the same nature. The same holds true for their relations with the regional school superintendent. We conclude that there is a duplication of duties and a duplication of communication. Add the possibility of conflict to this ambiguity and little more is needed to upset the official channels of communication. However, too faithful an adherence to procedures governing the communications between the different levels in the structure could result in the blocking of official channels."

In commenting on the problems faced by Indians in their quest for involvement in the education of their children, the Hawthorn report says: "As they [Indian people] are today, they constantly follow in the wake of administrative officers whose intentions they barely understand and over whom they have practically no control. For example, when Indians wish to make a complaint, they do not know to whom they should go, how to state their grievances or when to expect an answer.

Moreover, the local and regional officials are themselves incapable of solving most of the problems immediately. They are constantly obliged to refer to their superiors and wait for an answer to come from above. Very often this answer comes too late or is not the most appropriate solution. How often have officials in the field spoken to us about the pyramidal structure of school organization and have complained that decisions are taken by their superiors without prior consultation or without sufficient consultation with everyone involved. One could wish that decisions came from below and were afterwards ratified by the top officials of the organization."

If education is to be one means of breaking the shackles of Indian poverty, an entirely new pattern of authority must be initiated and education must be redefined to make it relevant to the needs and culture of the Indians of Canada. Education cannot operate in isolation from the people. Unless it is accompanied by adult achievement, it will have little meaning or appeal to the student. A programme slanted toward the needs of tomorrow cannot operate in the vacuum of yesterday and today.

The government's aims are so obviously geared to doing away eventually with our reserves that every programme offered by the government becomes suspect. Because our people recognize the overall aim of the government to take our lands from us, there is hesitancy to participate in any programmes offered by the government. The education programme, so obviously pointed toward assimilation, becomes doubly suspect. Assimilation would put an end to reserve life and thus make it simple for the government to conclude Indians no longer needed or wanted their homelands.

In its obsession with assimilation the government has denied the Indian the opportunity to make a choice as to whether he will live on a reserve or in an urban setting. Every man, Indian or non-Indian, should have some degree of choice as to his home environment, and opportunities must be found to permit fulfillment in modern society without necessarily requiring every man to become an urbanite.

For the Indian child education must help in the discovery of a positive self-image and must arm him with the skills that will help him survive in man's new wilderness—modern society. Discussions must be initiated immediately between the political leaders of Canada and our leaders to redirect and reshape the nature of Indian education. A total education for the total needs of the Indian people must be devised.

This involves a shift in power. As far as the political structure of our society will allow, the Indian people must have total control over the education of their children. The power to decide where children go for their schooling and how they will be educated must be transferred to our people. Parents must be the ones to decide what schools they want their children to attend. Band councils and local school boards or committees must work together in determining where new schools are located, in white or nonwhite communities.

As usual, the measure of participation and control by Indians advocated by the officials of the Department of Indian Affairs represents their typical reaction—too little, too late.

The concept of formal education must be expanded to include more of the needs of adult Indians. Educational institutions under Indian control and financed by government must be available to meet the training needs of our unskilled, untrained, unemployed adults. Special educational institutions must be created, under Indian control, to provide training in leadership at all levels. The Department of Indian Affairs does offer some courses in leadership training but for the most part they are irrelevant to our needs and opportunities. Where they do have some usefullness, their utility is negated by the suspicion that they are departmental brain-washing mills, turning out a new batch of Uncle Tomahawks.

Indian leaders and Indian organizations have now developed the capacity to handle such responsibilities. As a matter of fact they probably are the *only* ones equipped to meet the needs of our people in the area of specialized leadership training. Federal officials should see to it that money is provided for this purpose.

All new federal programmes for education, any further federal-provincial master agreements in education, anything relating to Indian education from now on must be arrived at with total Indian involvement. If this involvement is lacking, no agreement with any branch of government will be worth the wind needed to blow it away.

Indian involvement means Indian participation right from the initial discussion. The old way of presenting the Indian people with a series of agreements already arrived at by one or both levels of government is dead. Such procedures say to the Indian, "Here, approve our plan for your good." We no longer will accept that.

Many bureaucrats feel that Indians are not yet ready to assume control of the education of their children but, we ask, how could even the most stupid Indian create a worse mess than has been handed him by the missionaries and bureaucrats over the past one hundred years? As long as the government persists in using education for its own designs, education will continue to be an unpleasant, frightening and painful experience for Indian children who have little reason to like or be interested in school anyhow.

If changes are not made, and soon; if the control of education continues to be outside the sphere of the Indian people, the future of our people looks truly bleak.

What's the Use?

The Welfare Trap

Recently at a meeting on one of our isolated northern reserves, a young chief, bewildered and angered by his dealings with white authorities, sounded off about his experiences:

"Years ago our people were self-reliant. We made our living by trapping and from whatever nature was able to provide for us. Our life was hard. It was not an easy life—we had to use our minds continually to try and find means and ways by which to survive. But we lived like men.

"Then the government came and offered welfare to our people. They also tried to give a little money through which we were to start something by which to make a new type of livelihood. When they offered us welfare, it was as if they had cut our throats. Only a man who was crazy would go out to work or trap and face the hardships of making a living when all he had to do was sit at home and receive the food, and all he needed to live. It seemed as if the government had laid a trap for us, for they knew that once we accepted welfare they would have us where they wanted us.

"For a few years they provided welfare. During those years, our minds went to sleep, for we did not have to use them in order to survive. The years confused our minds. Then all of a sudden the government decided to cut off welfare assistance and also the economic development assistance that they were starting to provide. We found ourselves sitting in the middle of nowhere, for both our sources of survival had been taken from us and we had almost forgotten what it was like to make a hard living off the land.

"I think this is where the government made its mistake. The government officials are white, and they are smart, but they, too, can make mistakes. I think they made a mistake when they gave us welfare for they did not seem to think of its consequences. The next time the government does something it should think twice. If it wants to give us welfare, then it should be prepared to give it to us for the rest of our lives or otherwise leave us alone. I, for one, will not have anything to do with welfare, for if I were to take it, then they would think that they owned me. They would come back later and say, 'at such and such a time, I gave you welfare.' I could never be a free man. I would first starve to death before I asked for assistance from them.

"We do not want welfare assistance from the government. I would rather see the government put its money where it would help us most. There are resources in our land. There are some ways by which we could make a living. But we are Indians who are just emerging from the ways of trapping and hunting. We do not know the ways of the white man. We do not have the skills to make a living like the white man does. Instead of sending welfare, why does the government not send us men who would come and see our land, to see what forms of work it could provide? Why does the government not send us men who would come to teach us the skills we need to survive in the ways of the white man? Why does the government ignore our presence? Why do they not send men to sit down with us so that together we could lay down plans for the future of our people? Instead of sending us welfare, why does the government not send us the money to develop the resources that we have here so that people can make their living from these reserves?

"I think this would be better for our people. I think that this would help us regain our manhood. This is the only way that I can see for our people.

"Maybe I am wrong, because these are only my thoughts. But one thing I do know, we will never get anywhere, the way the government is working."

These thoughts, from a relatively young chief with little formal education, express the feelings and the thinking of the vast majority of Indian people in Canada. Each Indian petition, each Indian brief to the government of Canada has contained pleas for an alternative to welfare. Each group of Indians has its plans. Each band has its priorities. Even the uneducated Indian at the reserve level knows that resources are available and at least something of the potential of such resources. What he lacks is the human and financial help to develop that potential.

The government and white society have asked the Indian a million times over during the past century, "What do you want?" The Indian at first whispered and said, "This is what I want." But the government and white society did not listen. Then the Indian spoke up more boldly, but still no one listened. Now the Indian is screaming his wants, but still the government and white society do not listen. What does it take?

What the Indian wants is really quite simple. He wants the chance to develop the resources available to him on his own homeland, the reserve. What he needs to make this possible includes financial assistance, enough money to do the job properly so that he does not fail for lack of adequate financing; training in the precise skills he will need to develop the resources, training so practical and appropriate to the task that he will not fail because he does not have the know-how to do the job and, finally, access to expert advice and counsel throughout the stages of development so that he will not fail because he was given the wrong advice or no advice at all. With the money, the know-how and expert guidance, then if the Indian fails, at least it will not be because he didn't try to succeed and at least it will not be because he was not allowed to try.

One key factor remains, Indian involvement. Our people want the right to set their own goals, determine their own priorities, create and stimulate their own opportunities and development. The government knows this. This is part of what we have whispered, talked and screamed about. But the government mind, once on a path, seems difficult to divert. Once a government bureaucrat makes up his mind, there is no point trying to change it with logic and facts. And the government long ago decided it knew what was best for its Indian charges.

Government people, some of them admittedly with the best of intentions, continue to create their own pet projects for Indians, projects they argue earnestly are best for the Indian. They say, "Now, here's what we [meaning the government and the Indian] are going to do," then wonder why we aren't interested. They even say, lately, "We will consult you and involve you," but then they turn away in the presence of an Indian while they are doing their planning. When the plans are drawn up, they assume that because an Indian was in the room, or in the building or in the vicinity, he has been consulted and involved. They act indignant and bewildered when the Indian not only refuses to accept it as "his" plan but emphatically tells the white man what he can do with it. They say, "What is the use of trying to do anything for the Indian? He isn't interested."

Most people, Indian or white, realize there exists no simple, quick solution to the problems faced by the Indian people. No magic solution will wash away the social disorganization or the spectre of poverty. Three basic, fundamental factors hold the answer: development of strong Indian leadership, implementation of the total spectrum of education and the creation of a strong economic base. On the face of it, the vicious poverty that grips our people presents one of the most complex human problems that any society might face. But the very fact that the problem was man made argues that the solution does not lie beyond man.

Until now, however, the approach of the federal government to the problems faced by our people suggests a bewildered horse doctor. Because he doesn't know what he is doing, and because the last thing he will admit is that he doesn't know what he is doing, he scurries about surveying and resurveying the symptoms and prescribing piecemeal remedies. He never gets around to examining the causes of the ailment; consequently he never has the right remedy. Unfortunately the problem affects the horse even more than it does the doctor. The horse dies.

The Indian Affairs approach to education is at its best a disgrace to the principles of that institution and at its worst a disaster for the people who most need it and would benefit from it. Its tentative stabs at a leadership programme have lacked the first essentials of understanding. Similarly, the government approach to economic development is insane. The government is like the foolish man who sees his house rotting. Instead of repairing it or replacing it, he whitewashes it in order to make his gullible neighbour believe that all is well.

The approach to these difficulties must be that of a total, comprehensive plan arrived at in conjunction with our people and involving both societies. We must recognize as failures and do away with the piecemeal, schizophrenic measures advanced by the government up to now. The federal government has hopelessly imprisoned itself in an inward-flowing spiral that narrows its scope and range of alternatives. It has looked at the naked symptoms of poverty and has responded by allotting approximately twenty-five percent of its total budget to welfare, in contrast to about ten percent to economic development. It has become so involved in its welfare approach that it has been unable to see any alternative.

When a little bit of welfare doesn't work, it pours in more massive doses. When a few welfare workers can't contain the problem, the government heeds their call for more and yet more welfare workers, who in turn take one look and holler for *more* welfare workers. As this negative emphasis grows, more and more of the government's budget for Indians must be siphoned off to meet spiralling welfare costs, at the same time draining the needed financial and human resources for a positive economic development programme.

If one assumes that all the vast machinery of government and all its resources are needed to provide policies of economic development, education, welfare, land trusteeship, justice and so on to the citizens of Canada, then it becomes understandable that a single department trying to do all of these things for the Indians would run into difficulties. One single department of government, one ministry, because of its obligations to the Indians, in effect must serve as a complete minigovernment. Small wonder the Department of Indian Affairs has grown and multiplied frantically upon itself. It has been suggested that this department indeed has been so busy trying to manage its own growth that it never has had time to worry much about Indian growth. Indians long have agreed with Mr. Chrétien's present proposal to do away with the department, but never in the way he proposes to do it, by simply washing government hands entirely of the Indian.

The present economic development policies of the Department of Indian Affairs never will work, because they are upside-down policies. The local staff of the department attempts to identify the need of the people. From such a projection of needs the costs involved are forecast. Even carried out with the best of intentions, such procedures quickly expose two inherent flaws. The first is that, in the majority of cases, the planning and identification of needs fails to consider any local involvement. No one bothers to ask the Indians. Their problems and needs are assessed without their opinions. Secondly, the qualifications of the government officials making such projections are highly questionable. The junior officers responsible at the local level are persons who possess little or none of the background education necessary for the task. They seldom have, for example, the broad knowledge of economics necessary. In fact, often their only qualification is their years of dedicated service and unswerving loyalty to the regulations of their department.

From these first agency-level projections stem the department's regional forecasts and, from those, the department in Ottawa then calculates its budgetary needs on a national basis. By the time the branch in Ottawa gets to its budget, its projections are based on theoretical assumptions that do not relate to the realities of life in a reserve community.

Housing has been a major reserve problem for as long as anyone can remember. Belatedly, but finally, the government discovered this and even more belatedly set about doing something to alleviate the problem. Not long ago, on one northern reserve a survey team decided that a certain number of houses were needed. If the white man had to live in some of the Indian shacks on our northern reserves, it wouldn't take him long to agree. Indians on the reserve were delighted. Not only would they for the first time have decent, modern housing, but nearly every unemployed man on the reserve would find work helping to build the houses. The first disillusionment came with the arrival of the material for the houses. With the material came teams of white carpenters.

The second disillusionment followed quickly. As the houses took shape, the people could see they would offer little improvement upon the shacks they were to replace. When they complained, the agent said, "What do you expect, castles? The government only allots seven thousand dollars for each house."

The third disillusionment came with the completed housing. Before the end of a year, frames sagged, doors hung ajar and wouldn't close, windows wouldn't open, plumbing was out of line and wouldn't function, insulation against the wintry blasts of our northland slid down between walls which had sagged every which way. The reason? Quite simple. The houses had been built in the worst possible location on the reserve, squarely in the middle of the only swamp available. They had no foundations. Nearby Indian shacks, miserable as they were, at least stood solidly on firm ground, inadequate but intact. Whey didn't the Indians complain when they saw where the houses were being built? Are you kidding? They did. What happened? From the regional office over five hundred miles away, from a man who never had bothered to visit the reserve, came the word. "These houses will be built where designated or not at all." This man had determined the location by sticking his finger on a map.

The solution was panic. The government could only propose to send in engineers to drain the swamp and shore up the houses, at still greater expense. That is department planning.

There are white men who believe that the lack of economic advancement among Indians is caused by their unwillingness to grasp opportunities presented them. More, perhaps, believe that all Indians really want is handouts, a welfare existence. Some will tell you that the problem is simpler, that the Indian just naturally is too lazy to work or that Indians lack the imagination and creativity to do anything for themselves. No thinking could be more viciously stupid and wrongheaded.

At one reserve I know of, nearly all the people were on welfare. One day the Indian agent announced that welfare was not working on this reserve and that he was cutting it off. "Why give welfare to people who won't work when they have the opportunity?" he said.

We investigated. "What do you mean, the people won't work?" we asked.

"They have had all kinds of offers of jobs in the nearby communities and on nearby farms," the agent said, "and they just won't work. We see no point in continuing to support these lazy bums."

The agency solution was to move all the people from that reserve to another where there would be more opportunity for Indian farming. In order to force the people, who did not want to leave their homes, to move, not only was relief cut off but all forms of economic development assistance were stopped.

We asked the people on this reserve why they would not take the jobs the agent told us had been offered them. Their reply was that they were not slave labour. After checking further, we discovered that the jobs at stake paid about one-half to the Indians what the same employers would have paid for the same kind of work from their own people. We agreed with the reserve chief who told the agent they could take their jobs and shove them.

Lack of funds presents a continual problem to Indians who would like to get on with either personal or collective projects. Take the case of an individual Indian who wants to farm. He surveys the land available and decides that he needs twenty thousand dollars as a minimum to get his land cleared and the necessary machinery and facilities on the land. He goes to the government man and tells him that he wants to start farming. "Fine," is the answer, "go ahead." Then the Indian says he needs twenty thousand dollars. The government man has an easy answer: "We'll check into it." The real answer is that no funds are available. In some instances, where a revolving loan fund has been made available for Indian use, it is so small that there is never enough in it for practical use. Perhaps the agent will tell the would-be farmer, "We can get ten thousand dollars for you from the loan fund." Both know that to start a farming project with half the minimum requirement in financing is to ensure failure. More likely the agent will say, "We'll lease your land for you. There is no need for you to farm it. This way the man who leases it will clear it and save you all that cost; eventually, when the lessee leaves, you will be ready to have a go at it." But still the Indian can do no good. His land is cleared but he has no machinery and no opportunity to borrow enough to finance the machinery he needs. Then the agent says, "What's the use? The Indian can't do it." After ten or fifteen years of this sort of thing and after watching it happen to man after man, the Indian is likely to agree, "What's the use!"

Granted, there are a few cases where Indians have managed to get a start in farming or ranching. Even then difficulties lie along the path. Few Indians have received the kind of training a white farmer has for his work, the sort of training necessary in this age to make a go of a farm. The Indian realizes that farming has become a complex operation requiring knowledge of land use, of proper fertilization, of correct use of chemicals to clear out weeds or insects, an understanding of bookkeeping, some familiarity with marketing procedures. So he asks for expert counsel, guidance. What does he get? Some employee in the department who has the farm desk but has never been on a farm. I've seen expert advisors arrive on a farm who didn't even know wheat from barley.

On the majority of reserves there is economic development potential. Projects based on such potential could and should be initiated to give employment opportunities to the Indian people. Again I emphasize that such projects can hope to succeed only if they are launched after full consultation with the Indians and with full involvement of the people concerned. There are too few such projects in existence today, and the fault lies with the government rather than with the Indian. The government seems to expect the Indian to fail, indeed, sometimes seems almost disappointed if he doesn't. And there is the old bugaboo of government projects, perhaps well thought out, offered with the best of intentions, but simply imposed on the Indians by some theoretical genius in the department. Even when it is something that might work, there is a communications problem which the government either doesn't recognize or doesn't think worth the effort to solve. Many times I have sat and listened as government project officers presented such schemes to the people of a needy reserve. In beautiful, correct, professional terminology the government men go over the project point by point, forgetting they are talking to a people who sometimes find ideas expressed in English difficult. At the end of the explanation the government man adjusts his glasses, peers over his nose and asks, "Any questions?" Of course there are none. Not one of the people present has the faintest idea what in the hell the guy has been talking about. But the happy government man goes away saying, "There were no questions, so they must have understood." Then he blames the people when they show no interest in implementation of his pet project. "We tried to do what was best for them," he mumbles, "and where did it get us? Nowhere." How about letting the Indian, for a change, decide what is best for him? At least that would be a different approach.

Perhaps if more such projects were initiated by Indians, helped along by qualified white men, there would be less reason for the government to waste its money, time and good men in futile attempts to bodily transplant or relocate Indians in towns and cities. Two notable failures along this line have occurred at Elliott Lake and at Edmonton. Again well-meant, the projects involved the moving or relocating of a number of families from isolated reserves to a city. The families were provided with good modern homes. The wives were given special instruction in the care of such homes and were taught proper shopping techniques. The children were put into schools that were integrated, generally especially for them. Nurseries were provided for preschool tots. The men were given special on-the-job training and paid well while they learned their new skills.

All that was missing was the human element. Integration of the children was too abrupt. The change was too great for the women. They were not able to make white friends. The men were not carefully enough prepared for the new training and the new way of life. Each family became a little brown ghetto in its new environment, and one by one they slipped away, back to where they at least felt like human beings again.

Nothing but the white man's lack of vision stands in the way of Indians making successes of development projects right in their own communities. Both the federal and provincial governments could assist Indian communities in enticing industrial companies to locate close to or on reserves. Many manufacturing processes could function in such locations. Government help in the form of tax or transportation subsidies could make such relocation attractive. Government and Indian cooperation with such companies could provide training programmes to ensure a consistent and high-quality labour body right on the reserve.

In many cases individual Indian businesses could spring up to service the needs created by the presence of such a company. A provincial or federal Indian economic development corporation, under Indian control, could be established wherever necessary to provide the needed investment capital for the growth of Indian businesses and communities. Normal business procedures are all that would be required for the efficient functioning of such a development corporation. Because of restrictions written into the *Indian Act*, Indians always have had difficulty possessing or managing investment capital in sufficient amounts effectively to initiate any but the smallest of Indian-managed projects.

Indians also have suffered from inability to obtain sufficient and proper technical assistance for the success of their programmes. The expertise within the Department of Indian Affairs has proved to be nearly nonexistent. There is, however, no reason why Indians cannot open other channels of communication. Other departments within the federal government, top men from provincial governments, professional experts from Canada's universities and from private industry could be found. Indian organizations with full knowledge of the type of assistance required could be used to locate and hire such expert consultants as might be needed. Federal funds need not be wasted.

The emphasis of the present government development policies must be altered. Future policies in this vital area of Indian development must be based on a solid, realistic foundation designed to make the needed resources available in such a way that the Indian confidently and proudly can plan his own future. The area of socio-economic development has been neglected for over a century. What has been accomplished to date fails to add up even to a beginning.

In their mutual quest for better alternatives, the Canadian government and the Indians of Canada face great challenges and great opportunities. Socio-economic development offers on both sides of the Buckskin Curtain the challenge to utilize imagination and creativity in solving one aspect of a complex, unhappy situation.

Here to Stay

The Mystery of the White Man

An Indian, who probably wasn't joking at all, once said, "The biggest of all Indian problems is the white man." Who can understand the white man? What makes him tick? How does he think and why does he think the way he does? Why does he talk so much? Why does he say one thing and do the opposite? Most important of all, how do you deal with him? As Indians, we have to learn to deal with the white man. Obviously, he is here to stay. Sometimes it seems a hopeless task. The white man spends half of his time and billions of dollars in pursuit of self-understanding. How can a mere Indian expect to come up with the answer?

The white man has some good qualities. Over the centuries he has managed to work out some quite acceptable concepts of morality, justice, democracy, freedom, equality and so on, none of them new to the Indian, but all decent, solid thinking. But the white man is a paradox. On the one hand, he professes almost fanatic commitments to high ideals; on the other hand, he disdains those same ideals in practice. He believes in the concept of unity. He believes in a God and adheres to a monotheistic religion. Yet even in the area where he could offer most, in the one area where he could exemplify unity—in his religion—he is ridiculously fragmented. He preaches love and brotherly concern and manufactures napalm and hydrogen bombs—and who doubts he will use them?

The white man seems unable to understand, or perhaps he is unwilling to accept the fact that another man may believe differently, that another man's religion may be valid.

I know this is not a new discovery about the white man. But it continues to puzzle the Indian. The white man feels compelled to pray for the salvation of another's soul, and if that soul won't go along, just as compulsively condemns it to eternal damnation. And while he preaches brotherly love and tolerance, he often simultaneously directs his place of worship to become an all-white sanctuary.

In his social doctrines he stresses his belief in equality and elaborates on the need for and the value of diversity. But confront him with a diversity in colour of skin, confront him with some different values and see how long he stays a champion of diversity. He believes in equality, but apparently believes the white man is more equal than the Indian. He just doesn't make sense. Study of the white man will make a great field for future Indian psychologists and psychiatrists.

Much of the misunderstanding between white and Indian races in Canada arises because of basic ignorance about the differences between them. Some aspects of this difference are strongly developed in an article entitled, "American Indians and White People," by two leading anthropologists in the United States, Rosalie H. Wax and Robert K. Thomas:

"Social discourse is one of the areas where Indians and whites most easily misunderstood each other.... From childhood, white people and Indians are brought up to react to strange and dangerous situations in quite different ways. The white man who finds himself in an unstructured, anxiety-provoking situation is trained to react with a great deal of activity. He will begin action after action until he either structures the situation, or escapes from it, or simply collapses. But the Indian, put in the same place, is brought up to remain motionless and watch. Outwardly he appears to freeze. Inwardly, he is using all of his senses to discover what is expected of him—what activities are proper, seemly, and safe. One might put it this way: in an unfamiliar situation a white man is taught to react by aggressive experimentation—he keeps moving until he finds a satisfactory pattern. His motto is 'Try and try again.' But the Indian puts faith in observation. He waits and watches until the other actors show him the correct patterns....

"Perhaps it will be reassuring to the Indian to realize that the reckless torrents of words poured out by white people are usually intended as friendly, or, at least, social gestures. The more ill at ease a white man becomes, the more he is likely to talk. He is not nearly so afraid of making mistakes as is the Indian, and it is almost impossible (by Indian standards) to embarrass or 'shame' him. By the same token, he will rarely hold an Indian's mistakes against him...."

"In every human relationship there is some element of influence, interference, or downright compulsion. The white man has been and is torn between two ideals: on the one hand, he believes in freedom, in minding his own business, and in the right of people to make up their minds for themselves; but, on the other hand, he believes that he should be his brother's keeper and not abstain from advice, or even action, when his brother is speeding down the road toward perdition, death.... The Indian society is unequivocal: interference of any form is forbidden....

"Consequently, when the white man is motivated as his brother's keeper, which is most of the time when he is dealing with Indians, he rarely says or does anything that does not sound rude or even hostile to the latter. The white, imbued with a sense of righteousness in 'helping the downtrodden and backward,' does not realize the nature of his conduct, and the Indian cannot tell him, for that, in itself, would be 'interference' with the white man's freedom to act as he sees fit."

Wax and Thomas's findings are couched in general terms, but they describe meaningful differences in cultural approaches to everyday life which must be mutually understood if the Buckskin Curtain is ever to come down. Certainly they mean much more than the sweeping generalizations Indians have become so sick of hearing. "The Indian is irresponsible.... The Indian is lazy.... He is slow and lacks initiative.... The Indian is prone to liquor.... He has no one but himself to blame.... The Indian is morally lax.... The Indian can not be relied upon...." The myths persist. The biases and bigotry thrive. Those with the least knowledge always seem to have the biggest mouths. It is hard to believe but, even in this age of the moon walk, there are some who still maintain that the Indian is inherently, biologically inferior.

Despite the white man's righteous and indignant assertions that he has no feeling of prejudice against the Indian, we know that his true feelings surface when there is confrontation. We will believe the white man when his actions match his words.

Luckily Indians have resilience to match their stoicism. We will survive the stupidities of bigotry, the indignities of condescension and the gushing of the do-gooders, but we admit to deep and penetrating wounds inflicted by the white man's attitude toward our women.

The word *squaw* in Cree means woman (or lady, if you prefer that delicate locution). No Indian word has been so abused and perverted. On the white man's tongue, *squaw* is a dirty word used to describe any Indian woman. The connotation is one more appropriately drawn from the term *whore*, another white word our people dislike. To match our feelings when we hear our wives, mothers, sweethearts and daughters called squaws, lump your white wives, daughters, mothers and sweethearts under the general connotation of whore.

But you white men still are far ahead of us in actual abuse and perversion of our women, never mind the terminology. In too many areas Indian women are regarded by every passing stray white tomcat as easy prey. Nor is this attitude confined to white trash. Many God-fearing, good, solid, middle-class white citizens mouth self-righteous concern about the supposedly lax morals of Indians and at the same time conveniently overlook the actions of their fun-loving sons or brothers or husbands.

The despoilation of our women by unthinking, unfeeling, self-indulgent whites stands as the most degrading insult inflicted upon our people. The white social institutions of Canada seem blind to the situation. Turn the tables and see what would happen. Imagine a carousing invasion of one of your suburbs by roistering young Indian males in search of white girls for easy conquest. Like the white man's forked tongue, his morality comes in double standards.

We don't know where to start to correct this situation. The institution of the law might seem an appropriate place, but there is a saying among Indians: "If a white man rapes an Indian woman, he gets a suspended sentence or goes free, but if an Indian rapes a white woman he receives the lash and a sentence of life imprisonment." Aside from the implication that the double standard has pervaded the hallowed courts of Canadian justice, we might suggest that the comparative availability of high-cost legal aid to whites and to Indians represents another perversion of the concept of equality.

White people have a long way to go on this one. They might start by banning the use of the word *squaw*. Indian women are as moral as white women or women of any other colour. This is a cultural trait, an individual trait, not a race or colour characteristic. Our people had rigid moral codes before the white man found his way across the ocean. We will match our girls' character against your best team of debutantes any day.

Much has been written on prejudice. American bookstores are full of bitter and clever books by talented black authors. This is a step in the right direction, but it will take another several generations of goodwill and soul searching to wipe out the black or the red colour line.

From the beginning, the Indian accepted the white man in Canada. We allowed him differences. We helped him overcome his weaknesses in trying to make his way in our environment. We taught him to know our world, to avoid the pitfalls and deadfalls, how to trap and hunt and fish, how to live in a strange environment. Is it too much to ask the white man to reciprocate?

An Indian looks at nature and sees beauty—the woods, the marshes, the mountains, the grasses and berries, the moose and the field mouse, the soaring eagle and the flitting hummingbird, the gaudy flowers and the succulent bulbs. He sees an overall fitness, an overall collective beauty, but he looks deeper. He sees the beauty of the individual components of the big picture. He sees the diversity of the various elements of the entire scene. He admires the grace of a leaping deer, the straight-line simplicity of the pines the deer leaps through, the jagged, three-dimensional thrust into the sky of the rugged peaks, the quick silver flash of trout on the surface of a wind-rippled lake. He turns a sensitive ear to the faraway eerie wail of the loon and the nearer snuffling grunt of a bear pawing at a ground squirrel's den, and he blends them into the whispering of grasses and the bolder talk of the tall pines. He feels the touch of wind against his cheek and the coolness of the mist above the rapids. He surveys the diversities of nature and finds them good.

An Indian thinks this might be the way of people. He knows that whites and Indians are different. He knows that there are differences even within these larger groups, differences between Scot and Ukrainian, between Cree and Iroquois. He knows there are differences between man and his brother, red or white.

To the Indian this is the natural way of things, the way things should be, as it is in nature. As the stream needs the woods, as the flowers need the breeze, as the deer needs the grasses, so do peoples have need of each other, and so can peoples find good in each other. Indians are close to nature, so it is natural for them to see the bigger world in terms of the small world they do know. They know that men of different cultures and races have much to offer one another. We offer our culture; we offer our heritage. We know it is different from yours. We are interested in your culture and your heritage; we want you to discover ours.

Bring Back
the Medicine Man

The Missionary Fifth Column

If the Great Spirit is dead the Indian knows who killed him. It was the missionary. If the church is not dead it most certainly is dying, and the Indian knows what poison worked here, too—the missionary.

If there is still a place in modern-day Indian society for the church, that place must be found and designated by the Indian. The church is so discredited in native society that quite possibly its smartest move in the long run would be to cease all its activities on behalf of native peoples. After a time, provided a new approach relates to the spiritual and moral needs of our people, the church might be able to find a new purpose and acceptance.

Even Indian folklore notes that long ago Indians sent the Great Spirit across the oceans to take their religion to the godless white man and that the white man killed him. Other Indian legends, handed down from father to son for generations around the campfire, differ in detail but generally tell of the creation of the world and all the animals and living things on it, and of man. They relate the story of the virgin birth of a spiritual leader, the story of the great flood and they tell of the triumph of the spirit of good over the spirit of evil in a great battle. Long before the white man came to the new world, Indians held ceremonies of thanksgiving and of spring's coming. There were sacrifices and offerings and prayers to win favour or appease the spirits. There was the shared suffering with the Great Spirit that came with the self-torture of the sundance and other religious ceremonies.

True, not all Indians were monotheistic; many attributed spirit or soul to everything animate and many things inanimate, but nearly all shared concepts of a Great Spirit dominating all other spirits. Whether he was called Manito, Orenda or Wakanda, the Great Spirit of the Indian was much like the Mana of the Polynesian or the God of the white man.

The Indian believed in the spirit of brotherly love, in the principle of sharing, in the purification of giving, in the good sense of forgiving.

The Indians developed prophets and seers who were akin to holy men, who served their people as healers and sorcerers, who were both good and evil. These were the medicine men.

The medicine men held great power in the Indian society. A medicine man of strong character quickly became a social and political leader of his people as well as a spiritual advisor. In a modern white village he would be a combination of the mayor, the local general practitioner and the local minister of the only church in town. He was the renaissance man of the Indian society.

He was the man of God, the go-between serving both the Great Spirit and the people. He proclaimed the taboos; he interpreted visions and dreams; he led the ceremonies of blessing and propitiation and all the people's prayers.

He was the doctor who healed with herbs or with the laying on of hands. He knew which roots to grind for the man with a cold; he knew which leaves made the best poultice for the man with a running sore; he knew which herbs, properly smoked, did the same work the Pill does today when an Indian family couldn't afford more children and which to give when natural fertility needed a jolt. For every disease he had a plant, a berry, a root, a herb; he was part doctor, part pharmacist and certainly a great naturalist.

With his arduously acquired powers over both the natural and the supernatural, the medicine man was both greatly respected and greatly feared. In fact, there was little more fearsome to an Indian than a medicine man with a bent toward evil. Spells and poisons were great medicine, too. Normally, however, any medicine man's dark powers were focussed against members of enemy bands and only enhanced his local standing, especially when they triumphed. His experience and knowledge—medicine men usually were apprenticed while still adolescent and spent the remainder of their lives storing up the facts they had to know —and his guidance were sought by the band's political leaders; often, he was the real power behind the throne.

A good medicine man served as a sort of social stabilizer. Children were brought up to respect him and, through him, all their elders. A smart crack by a youngster always resulted in a swift cuff on the ears.

Because the medicine man's powers to reward correct behaviour were equalled only by his dark powers to punish incorrect behaviour, both youth and adults maintained a healthy respect for him. Children grew up on stories of the exploits of good medicine men. Such stories made their medicine men seem as heroic as Glooscap or Nanibush or Wisakedjak but without the unfortunate propensity for tricks those rather comic legendary heroes cultivated. Because most medicine-man legends stressed the triumph of his good or socially acceptable actions over his evil or socially disruptive side, he served as a social force for good. This was his position in the period before the coming of the missionary.

The first missionaries found the way almost prepared for them. They received a warm reception from the heathens and savages who weren't, after all, so heathenish or savage that they didn't welcome the message of a loving Jesus. The Indian was the first member of the ecumenical movement. He was willing to accept the white missionary's message of love for his fellow men, because it came as a complement to rather than a contradiction of the Indian way of life. The fact that the missionary lived with the people, shared their hardships, learned their language, suffered with them when the hunt was unsuccessful and rejoiced with them when things went well proved a tremendous asset in his work of conversion. Because he lived as one of them, the early missionary was able to move easily into the position of medicine man and was able to take over most of his roles. The new values brought by the white man seemed similar to their own and the Indians trusted their new teachers, put great faith in their message. The missionary became the new social and moral conscience of the Indian.

Because of the missionary's position in the band, he was able to ease the way for the coming of the fur trader, the settler, the white police, the new law bringers. Since he was a part of the new force, the missionary gradually took over the medicine man's role as law enforcer. With his cachet of medical aids, more sophisticated than those of the medicine man, he took over the final stronghold of the now-deposed tribal leader.

Certainly for the first generation of converts, the switchover from indigenous beliefs to those of Christianity was relatively smooth. The advance work by the missionaries enabled the churches to move in and carry on what amounted to immersion courses in their respective faiths. The transition was smooth for the Indians since none of their beliefs were stretched too far in the new direction. They dovetailed rather than clashed.

But the white missionary did not come, pure and simple, in the spirit of brotherhood. He came stealthily in the spirit of Christian brotherhood, a different concept. He came to preach his way and to convert, and he cared little even when he understood that his way disrupted the savage society.

As the missionary gradually pushed his only rival, the medicine man, out of the teepees and lodges, he began to introduce his own European value system. The missionary and the trappers and settlers who followed him laughed at the Indian version of religion, scoffed at the all-important visions and dreams, defied the ancient taboos without visible harm and brought with them dread new illnesses like smallpox, measles and influenza, which no combination of medicine-man herbs, roots and berries could cure.

The white religion was a religion of concern with the hereafter; the Indian way was more concerned with the practical everyday interplay of action between man and his familiar spirits. Slowly the Indian found the new faith perverting his ancient beliefs from a religion of action in everyday life to a religion of thou-shalt-nots. The new religion focussed on abstractions; the old religion had been oriented toward people. The old religion of the Indian's forefathers slowly was twisted into moral positions that had little relevance to his environment, twisted to fit seemingly senseless white concepts of good and bad. Pragmatic ethics and the morality enshrined in the Indian's code by his environment were replaced with a concern for good and evil that was foreign to the Indian.

The missionaries, either Roman Catholic or Anglican in the early days, were horrified when they learned that the medicine men were dispensers of birth control means. And they found other pagan practices to preach against. They scoffed at Indian offerings to lesser gods; they mocked propitiation of the spirits of animals killed for food or fur; they scorned the medicine man's posturing and costumes.

Some Indians felt that their old gods were better for Indians and the new ones better for white men but, generally, the Indian who clung to the old ways was left behind. He was denied the medicine of the old ways because the medicine man, once all-powerful, was stripped of his authority. An Indian's refusal to accept the new, stronger medicine of the white man left him, too, naked and defenceless.

The Indian was forced to put his trust in the new white medicine man. But when the missionary shoved the old medicine man aside he failed to fill all of the void left. He disrupted Indian society by removing from it the checks and balances that had been maintained under the old system. The missionaries' treatment of the second generation of Indian converts began to show a marked difference.

The missionary was there to convert the Indian. To convert him he had to care for him. To care for him in modern terms meant to educate the illiterate, leaderless Indian youth. The government shrugged aside responsibility for Indian education, quite content to let the church do the job. So it happened that the early spiritual goal was translated into educational objectives that proved disastrous to the Indian. The church's idea of education never progressed far beyond simply training the Indian to make him an easier convert.

The church, following the missionary into the Indian community, worked hand in hand with existing government officials in plotting the life of the Indian. There was a state of interdependence between the forces of church and government. The government needed the church to control the Indians by persuading them to live peacefully on reservations and encouraged the church to assume full leadership responsibilities. The church needed the power of the government to ensure that law enforcement powers would be at their disposal to force children to attend the residential schools churches were setting up. The churches further persuaded the government to pass legislation outlawing remnants of surviving Indian religious ceremonies, thus speeding conversion. The *Indian Act* of the 1920s and 1930s thus contained legislation forbidding some aspects of the sundance and the potlatch.

Collusion of church and state was supposed to facilitate the development of good Christian brown white men. The churches' perverted interest in education resulted in the neglect of the spiritual needs of the Indian communities. The development of the residential school system eroded the vital Indian family unit. Propagation of Christian beliefs rather than the dispersal of knowledge aimed at teaching the Indian to adjust to the new non-Indian society became the educational goal of the church schools.

Residential school was no bed of sweet balsam for the young Indian student. Often as early as the age of five, he was yanked forcibly from his parents' arms and taken scores of miles away to the residential school, where a system of harsh discipline combined with an utterly foreign environment quite literally left him in a state of shock. No effort was made to ease his introduction. He was jerked out of his bed at six o'clock in the morning, made to kneel at the side of his bed to thank God, presumably for letting him sleep until six, marched army fashion to communal washrooms, then to a chapel for morning prayers, back to a school dining hall where he had to listen to interminable Latin or English graces before he could touch the rapidly cooling gruel on the slab table before him. Then it was back to his room for half an hour. He hadn't been allowed to speak once up to now, and all too soon he had to march to a cold, cheerless classroom where the day started with still more prayers. So it went, daylong and day after day—march to lunch, march to play periods of half an hour each afternoon, march to bed by eight o'clock.

The children were not allowed to speak in their own language. Their teachers, unlike the early missionaries, made no attempt to understand the native tongue. They couldn't even be bothered to learn the children's names and gave them instead easier-to-pronounce Christian names.

No attempt was made to gauge the effect of this sort of life upon the pupil. If the priest-teachers knew of the anthropological evidence which even then suggested that Indians have a different time sense than whites (as do some creative people, Arabs, and Australian and African aborigines), they paid no heed. Alienation from his people and self-alienation was just one ramification of the regimented life of the residential school.

The priest-teachers seldom were qualified educators. Their goals didn't require that they be. All they wanted of their Indian charge was to pound a little English into his head, just enough to enable him to decipher religious materials, and to give him enough simple arithmetic to enable him to count the animals on the church farm. They didn't really care if they broke his spirit as long as they got the right responses at mass. If an Indian completed grade eight before he reached the age of sixteen, which wasn't often, he was given menial jobs on the farm attached to the residential school. Ostensibly he was learning the skills of farming or animal husbandry, to enable him to follow that vocation when he graduated.

Any initiative a young Indian might have had when he started through the church school system was beaten out of him before he finished. Rules and regulations counted for everything and discipline was severe. Such an environment conditioned the student to act only under strictly controlled circumstances. When he left the institution he was unable to function in an environment where initiative was needed to guarantee survival.

The churches were mistaken in thinking such a system would result

in lasting converts. Instead, each succeeding generation that struggled
through the residential schools reacted more violently against the
churches and against religion. Students identified the stern, repressive
and, at times, questionable disciplinary actions of the religious administrators with concepts of Christianity. Such abstract concepts as democ-
✓ racy and freedom meant nothing to the children even when attempts
were made to teach them, because there was no semblance of those concepts in the educational environment.

Let it be acknowledged that the missionary teacher acted (usually)
out of the best motives but brought about the worst of all results: a
Christian without character. By taking the child through his formative
years, the church school deprived him of the social training he would
have received at home and needed in order to fulfill his responsibilities
to his kin and to members of his society. He was deprived of the opportunity to learn his role and his relationship to members of his community. He was turned toward a life that was foreign to him and one that
he could not be a part of. But he was a stranger to his people upon his
return. The child went to school an Indian. The young man emerged a
✓ nothing.

To compound the damage, the missionary confronted the Indian with
a strange and bewildering array of white truths. He came to the Indian
carrying one bible in his hand, but he came carrying a hundred inter-
pretations of that bible in his head. The Roman Catholic, the Anglican,
the various other denominations of protestant faith that eventually
joined in, each went to the Indian with the same claim: "Our way is the
right way; to follow another path is to take a short cut to hell."

For religions that purportedly preached brotherly love and tolerance,
their actions bore no resemblance to the doctrinal wares they hawked.
Instead of engendering Christian love and consideration they encouraged divisiveness and bitterness even between members of the same
community. Since education became a conversion tool, each denomina-
tion or sect competed bitterly for the right to run individual schools.
Many Indian communities still bear the divisive scars.

The partnership of church and state also victimized the Indian.
Increased investment of time, money and people in his education forced
the churches to seek a role in government policy making. As their
involvement grew, their interests expanded. Churches unashamedly
used the plight of the Indian as a bargaining point with government
representatives, but conflicting pleas for money soon became pleas for

power. Even well-intentioned churchman-politicians came to believe that they and they alone could make the proper decisions for the Indians. No one asked the Indian.

Whether or not the churches today have the honesty to admit their responsibility for many of the social problems that exist in the native world, the Indian still accuses them. In their squabbling scramble for power the churches forgot the purpose of their presence in the Indian's world. They tore down the Indian social structure, but instead of erecting a new edifice they used the grounds as a parking lot of beliefs.

The tragedy amounts to much more than wasted opportunity. What the church has done may well be irreversible.

Churches can attempt to fill the void they have created by returning to their original purpose—fulfilling the spiritual and moral needs of the people. A decision of this nature means the renunciation of the educational and political aspects of their Indian responsibility. There is little evidence the churches are considering this or even realize the necessity. In fact, their involvement seems to be increasingly political. This makes their problem doubly difficult since the church today, any church, is not received into native society with the open arms which greeted the early missionaries. The approach must be different. Today the church faces a generation of Indians who are, to say the very least, sceptical of the church's sincerity, and who are at best dubious about any future role for it in their world.

In McLuhanish terms their approach must be *cool*; it must come from the heart as well as the head. It won't be easy. The church no longer has Indian trust. The temptation to tell the church to look to its own house first remains strong. From an Indian point of view the church has pretty well botched its white responsibilities, too.

The alternative is for the church to yield up its considerable influence upon our fate and to encourage the restoration of native beliefs and religions. Many Indians once again are looking toward the old as the hope of the future. Many Indian leaders believe a return to the old values, ethics and morals of native beliefs would strengthen the social institutions that govern the behaviour patterns of Indian societies. But would the Christian churches have the guts to get out? It seems highly unlikely. They still prefer sectarianism to faith.

They Know Not What They Do

The White Role in Red Society

Perhaps the time has come for a counterproposal to those non-Indians who think gallons of white paint liberally applied would solve the so-called Indian problem. Let the Indian in turn splash buckets of brown paint on the hordes of happy but ignorant white do-gooders who clutter up the Indian landscape. In short, the time has come to tell such innocently dangerous souls, "get brown or get lost." The sad truth is that there is just no way these well-intentioned people can do more good in the Indian community than by leaving it.

We acknowledge that there are many white people who have a genuine interest in what happens to the Indian. They really want to help. But they don't know how and their best efforts only muddy the waters. The big problem for the concerned non-Indian is simply that he doesn't know what he is doing. He lacks any clear understanding of the Indian and because of this he can't develop any clear perspective of the issues facing our people. His efforts confuse the issues rather than contribute to happy resolutions.

Since such people have hurt Indians more than they have helped them, the Indian people view the role of such non-Indians with suspicion, bitterness and scepticism. Such apprehension often and quickly turns to outright hostility. Indian terms for such people are paradoxically uncomplimentary in view of the interest they show and in light of their good intentions.

Unfortunately, these do-gooders get involved in spheres of activity ranging from simple, charitable church projects to the political arena, where self-appointed spokesmen for the Indians do incalculable harm. Their view of the Indian almost always, even if subconsciously, is that native people are incapable of handling their own affairs. The assumption that they must become actively involved in order to protect the Indian from himself follows naturally. We don't for a minute question the sincerity of these people, but we have to be realistic. It is our lives they are playing with. We do have to examine their role in the light of its potential effectiveness. We must ask them to do the same. We must ask that a non-Indian who is sincere show a little more sense of judgement. What he does or attempts to do must nourish the initiative of the Indian people. What he attempts must not discourage or inhibit the growth of individual potential. He must not set himself up as a decision maker for the Indian.

Such people can't seem to get it through their heads that the simplest and most important thing they can do is simply to accept the Indian for what he is, another human being, and treat him with the same consideration they would show any other individual.

All too often the do-gooder carries the virus of bigotry where he goes. While the typical do-gooder would swear on a stack of oil stocks that he does not believe that Indians are in any way inferior, his actions and his statements suggest a subconscious philosophy that even he may not be aware he harbours. But it shows and, like being a little bit pregnant, being a little bit bigoted is too much.

Quite unintentionally, the average non-Indian can fall into the cycle of paternalism. Take a typical, charitable, well-meant do-gooder project. A member of a women's church auxiliary has read in the local press or seen an item on television that certain Indians are running around barefooted in the snow because they are destitute or can't send their kids to school because the seats are out of their pants.

"Terrible, terrible," she clucks. "Absolutely scandalous; we can send three men to the moon but we can't keep our own Indians in decent clothes." So the good ladies get together. Each one paws through her closets and comes up with some clothing that is perhaps outgrown but still usable, perhaps some that the family simply has grown tired of and, really to turn her conscience on, even an item or two of practically new clothing. Then she goes around in a do-gooder glow for days. What did she actually do to earn such a glow? Perhaps she rummaged through a few closets, maybe made a few phone calls; she might even have helped pack the stuff for shipping one morning. So, okay, the stuff was needed; it might even prove useful. But are such people entitled therefore to feel they have made a private peace with the Indians? They must somehow be made to realize they have a deeper responsibility as citizens. Indians do not enjoy scrounging; they don't want to continue having their clothing bundled in to them, secondhand. While native people may truly appreciate whatever assistance they receive, they would appreciate far more efforts which would enable them to provide for the needs of their own families.

We understand full well and are sorry that the good ladies are hurt and upset when we fail to kiss their hands in humble, grateful thanks. But we suggest that they and all the others like them, those who do less and those who do more, take a deeper look at the situation. They can avoid the frustration that comes with apparent rejection of their lofty motives if they will take the time and make the effort to understand more deeply the temperament of the native people and the issues involved. Too many times the interested non-Indian assumes the role of an overpossessive mother who feels she must go on overprotecting her only child, must go on making decisions the child should be allowed to make. We are big boys now; we don't want to be mothered. Even if we suffer because we make wrong decisions, we would rather have mother suffer a little with us (if she insists) than have her deny us the choice.

It is time for concerned whites to reassess their involvement in a deep and honest manner so that their interest may become more meaningful to the native people. They must learn to accept criticism and even resentment of their actions as an attempt by those they would help to assure maximum returns from their activities.

The hard truth remains that the responsibility for the revitalization of the Indian society falls upon the shoulders of the Indian people and no one else. It is the Indian leaders, Indian organizations and the Indian people themselves who have the duty to explore new social and economic alternatives. For non-Indians truly to be effective there must be a clearer understanding of the respective areas of responsibility. The Indian's responsibility must be recognized and respected by the non-Indian, and it must not be shirked by the Indian himself.

Non-Indians have no business trying to organize the Indian people. Such would-be helpers go into Indian communities with predetermined and, inevitably, mistaken conclusions about problems and solutions. The theories held by these amateur sociologists seldom are related to the realities of Indian life and nearly always are irrelevant to the real problems.

On a more grandiose scale, some white idealists really believe they can reach an understanding of the people and assist specific Indian communities on the basis of summer field projects, perhaps spread over two or even three years. They have struck out before they take the field. Cultural differences are magnified by their approach. It will take many years of practical experience before the white man can comprehend fully the deep differences in the values of the Indians and those of middle-class Canadians. Even a lifetime of involvement by a dedicated white man does not always guarantee sufficient understanding to enable the non-Indian, however concerned and well meaning, to organize Indians for some form of social action. The history of non-Indian involvement shows again and again that just as whites begin effectively to relate to Indian communities, circumstances force them to move to other locations, breaking off the relationship just when it might have begun to pay off. Years are required before non-Indians can build a relationship of trust and confidence between themselves and the local Indian communities. There exists a suspicion toward whites in Indian communities. Regrettable or not, this distrust is a fact, and it plays a negative role when a white tries to get something started in an Indian community.

There is a tendency on the part of super do-gooders to work up all sorts of projects for Indian communities without ever consulting the community concerned. The agency or organization involved takes a superficial look, decides unilaterally what is needed or what will be good for the community and tries to transfer enthusiasm to the people. The Indians aren't asked, don't want and refuse to cooperate. When the project inevitably fails, bitter whites say that Indians aren't interested in change, or revolution, or whatever. They overlook the fact that it never was an Indian project and never could hold Indian attention; the Indians are busy with their own plans for change.

There is one way the whites can help, a way so simple that it generally is rejected out of hand. As the old comedian said, "Don't just applaud, send money." I would add, money without strings attached. While the responsibility for solutions rests with the Indian, there exists a shortage of resources with which he can meet his challenge. Money is one answer: money to enable organization leaders to travel, to enable them to meet with local peoples and their representatives for grass-root assessments; money to hire specialists in all fields—sociologists, economic experts, engineers—professional people we don't yet have in our own ranks. The solutions to the social and economic difficulties of the Indians depend upon our own ability to forge the type of resource teams we need and upon the extent to which we can build a genuine partnership with helpful resource people in the white community. Such professional people, as hired consultants, are desperately needed. More and more Indians recognize that, but those people cost money.

The effectiveness, then, of white people in Indian communities is highly questionable. Most Indian leaders will go a step further and say there just is no way the white man can be useful in that context. However, they can play a useful role in the non-Indian communities. There exists a great need for knowledge in the white society about Indians and similarly a need in Indian communities for more information about white society. Indian leaders stand ready to outline to whites the difficulties they see facing their people and to explain their own solutions. Interested whites can get this sort of information and pass it on to their own communities. As interest and understanding grow, as Indian-educated non-Indians educate their own people, more intelligent assessments can be made, more intelligent help offered. The kind of help and information Indians encountering white society need will then be more readily available. A basis for mutual understanding can develop.

The Indian people of Canada are convinced, after many bitter experiences with the federal government, that the situation in the latter part of the 1960s is different only in surface detail from the situation that existed in the nineteenth century. Then the Indians were the victims of unscrupulous traders, profit-swilling bootleggers and ignorant settlers. Today the Indians are victims of the mandarins in Ottawa who come to us as the Madison Avenue counterparts of the unholy trinity of the nineteenth century.

But if white society will accept a role that permits Indians to determine their own solutions for the future, if the whites will work among themselves to broaden their knowledge of the non-Indian society, such interested white people can and will play a crucial role in assuring racial stability in Canada. If Indians generally continue to remain ignorant of the situation facing the native Canadian, then Indians will continue in futile struggle against a government which has a history of betrayal and monumental bad faith.

Hat in Hand

The Long Fight to Organize

The time is nine o'clock any morning in the past. The setting is the outer office of the Indian agent at any reserve headquarters. An elderly Indian enters. The clerk looks up from his desk where he is reading last night's paper. He knows the man, and he knows what he wants. The clerk spent an hour yesterday talking to the agent about the old man and the agent had been explicit about how he was to be handled. The Indian waits at the chest-high counter. He is dressed in worn moccasins, blue jeans long-since faded, pale and dirt streaked, an old plaid wool shirt and a black suitcoat. Carefully he takes off his high-crowned broad-brimmed black hat and lays it on the counter, then picks it up and holds it uncertainly in one hand.

His family is hungry. There is little food in the old man's house. His welfare checks don't cover all that is needed. He has talked to some of the young men on the reserve about an Indian organization which would help people like him, but the agent tells him that only the government can help him. Now the time for trapping has come again, and he would be working and off relief for a few months if his traps were favoured and the fur prices were good. But he needs a loan, some money for traps. All the Indians know that the agent is empowered to disburse funds for traps, but all Indians also know that this is a discretionary power.

The clerk motions the Indian to one of the straightback chairs against the wall and returns to his paper. The old man waits to see the agent until a few minutes before five o'clock, when he is ushered into the agent's office by the clerk. The agent has his hat and coat on, ready to go home. He looks at his petitioner in distaste, as though it is the old man's fault he isn't already on his way home. The agent says, "I hope you understand now that the government is your only friend." The Indian says nothing, and the agent nods to the clerk. "You don't have to hang around here all day," he tells the Indian. "You'll get your trap voucher." The clerk motions to the Indian to come with him. In the clerk's office the necessary arrangements are made in a few minutes. The old man leaves the office at five-fifteen. He knows that he could have completed his business and left at nine-fifteen that morning. He knows that the agent kept him waiting just to show him who was boss, but he also knows there was no other way he could get the traps he needed to go to work again. The agent holds dictatorial powers over him and they both know it. That night when the young men come to talk to the old man about an Indian organization, he listens.

One of the most painful lessons that Indian peoples are learning is the need for organization through which they can articulate their needs and their alternatives to the Canadian society and its government. If the situation of the Canadian Indian is to be altered, even alleviated, the central issue is the degree of sophistication that we can develop in creating organizations which are Indian controlled and representative at the reserve level.

The work of creating stable and representative organizations has been one of the most difficult challenges faced by our people. It is a task that has always drawn the attention of Indian leaders in the past, and it is primarily because of their courage in attempting to meet this responsibility that things have changed for the better as much as they have.

The average Canadian is unaware of the work that has been done and is now being undertaken by Indian leaders, largely because the government has had access to the news media and the Indian people haven't. The government carefully has doled out truthful information about the actual conditions faced by our people, but it has buttressed this with mountains of propaganda celebrating their own noble efforts and programmes aimed at curing such conditions. The ordinary Canadian gets the impression that the fault for the situation rests with the Indian, because he is either unable or unwilling to take the opportunities provided by the benevolent Canadian government.

During the past forty or fifty years there have been innumerable attempts to develop organizations through which the Indian people could express their desires and through which they could suggest plans for the future to the Canadian society and its government.

In the 1920s serious attempts were made by Indian leaders to organize their people so that action could be taken to alleviate their plight. These courageous leaders sought to act positively to solve their problems in spite of overwhelming difficulties. Many factors beyond their control worked against their success. The transportation system of their day made it almost impossible for them to gather people together from across the country. No matter where a meeting was held in this vast land, days of travel by horse and wagon were required of some of the delegates. Poor communications made it extremely difficult even to get word to all areas about a proposed meeting. There was no money to pay the delegates' expenses. But perhaps the most difficult task was simply that of convincing the ordinary Indian that such an organization was worth the bother. Such social structures were alien to the Indian way. The older Indians, often those with influence in their communities, saw such organizations as a waste of time. The majority were illiterate and could not be convinced with printed material.

The Indian agent, dead set against any successful Indian organization, actively worked against the leaders of the day. To the autocratic agent who enjoyed making an Indian sit uselessly all day in an office the development of Indian organizations was a threat to his power and potentially to his job. He had many weapons and never hesitated to use them. Sometimes he openly threatened to punish people who persisted in organizational efforts. More often he used more subtle weapons such as delaying relief payments or rations to show the Indians which way the wind was blowing.

If the Indian leaders of the day were too active, they were labelled dangerous rabble rousers and were subjected to harassment by the police. By spreading gossip or falsifying facts, the government officials often were able to undermine the leaders through their own people. It was made quite obvious to people on the reserve that it was not wise to talk to certain Indians. These first leaders were genuine heroes. They had guts and they needed them. They had no money; they had no access to skilled and trained advisors; they were harassed by the white government officials and the police and they were doubted by their own people. Yet they fought on.

The work of organizing was complicated by the fact that it had to be done entirely on a voluntary basis. The Indian leaders spearheading the work had no resources but their own; they had no money for consultants and no help in the documentation of facts necessary to present their case.

Under these conditions, growth of Indian organizations was slow and difficult. The wonder is that there was any growth at all. However, although progress was slow, a basis for later organizational work was laid through the diligence and sacrifice of the leaders.

From the thirties to the mid-forties, development work of the early leaders began to pay off in the growth of Indian groups on a provincial basis. During these times some of the church leaders had begun to take an active interest and were encouraging their Indian parishioners to participate in organization work. Except for the odd meeting of individuals, the provincial organizations developed at this time in parallel but isolated circumstances. At this stage the first attempts were made to develop a national Indian organization. Largely because of geographical isolation and the lack of money, this effort, while moderately successful, did not take firm hold. However, the exercise was not wasted. It did awaken provincial Indian organizations to the existence of other, similar groups in other provinces, and the potential that lay in combined forces was apparent to everyone.

In fact, the provincial movements of that time were significant in that they gradually began to penetrate the isolation of the Indian communities. They assisted and encouraged local people to begin looking beyond the boundaries of their own reserves and areas. Through this opening up, they began to discover common problems. This led naturally to cooperation in seeking solutions to their problems. The leaders from far-separated reserves were able to learn from each other. In the exchange of ideas the new leaders were able to discard approaches that failed to work elsewhere and settle on those that experience had proven successful. The first efforts between reserves to help each other grew from such provincial meetings. Intertribal communication posed a major difficulty, but the use of interpreters and the commonly understood English language solved this problem.

As meetings began to develop a consistent pattern, the issues faced by the Indian people began to be defined more clearly and alternatives were presented more forcefully. The Indians began to express their concern for their rights, especially those upon which they depended for their livelihood. Nearly all were knowledgeable about such rights as hunting, trapping and fishing. The Indian people sincerely if mistakenly believed that their treaties or their rights were secure, for the federal government itself or the queen's representatives had made sacred promises. They united in opposition to increasing attempts to infringe upon or restrict those rights.

The leaders of the developing provincial organizations grew increasingly concerned with the lack of educational opportunities for their children, for they knew that this was to be one of the crucial problems. In education lay the future of their people.

Community leaders began to express their desire for some form of economic development. They realized that it was through this channel they would make the transition to a new environment, to a world that had changed without them.

The organizations began to take on more importance to the ordinary Indian. As they gained strength they were able slowly to lift the oppressive control of autocratic government representatives. No agent could with impunity keep an old man sitting idly all day in his outer office any more.

As the leaders examined their treaties and the rights that had been pledged on a government's honour, they began to discover the wide discrepancy that had developed between the treaties as they understood them and the perverted administration that was created to implement the terms of the treaties. They discovered for the first time that the legislation called the *Indian Act* and the administration they knew as the Indian Affairs Branch were in no way part of those treaties and that the spirit of the treaties was in fact never envisioned or contained in the legislation and administration created by the Canadian government.

With the postwar period came strengthening of the Indian organizations and increased pressure for more freedom from control by the Indian agents, for better educational opportunities, for more emphasis on resources to develop the communities and, most important, insistence upon the honouring and implementation of the terms of the treaties and the settlement of outstanding land claims.

As a direct result of the increased activity of Indian organizations, the Canadian government began to shift its course of action. Largely because of pressure from Indian leaders, in 1951 the Canadian government made its first attempt to change the *Indian Act*, an act that was created without the involvement of Indians and legislation that had not been altered significantly for fifty years. Indian pressure forced the government into action in two vital fields, education and health. For the first time the government took a serious look at its educational responsibilities. The health services, which were nearly nonexistent, were upgraded. The Indian organizations gained rapid strength until the mid-fifties. Their success came entirely from the determination and initiative shown by the Indian leaders. They got no help from the government.

A number of developments in the mid-fifties resulted in a setback for the growth of Indian organizations.

In western Canada, the agitation for better education facilities and opportunities had exposed the terrible inadequacies of the church-operated residential schools. In an effort to better the situation the government, under continuing pressure from the Indian organizations, was seeking alternatives to the moribund system. The churches, which initially had supported the Indian organizations, found themselves threatened in this area of vital concern—education. They promptly reversed their stand and withdrew their support of the Indian organizations. The Roman Catholic church went a step further than the other denominations. Not only did they pull back their support, they proceeded to set up something called the Catholic Indian League. Ostensibly this new organization was supposed to be concerned with the spiritual and temporal welfare of young Catholic Indians. While the CIL supposedly devoted its energies to the encouragement of religious vocations among the younger Indians, its obvious concern was the education of the Indian children through the residential school system. The wholly predictable effect of the organization of the Catholic Indian League by the clergy of that church was to divide the Indian people. By creating yet another organization the church weakened the base of the legitimate Indian organizations, attracting from them many Catholic members. Furthermore, the church's action increased the possibility of division among the Indians on religious lines.

This divisive move of the Catholic church may have been made innocently, without conscious intent to weaken the Indian organizations. Divisions along religious lines might not have been foreseen. The fact remains that the creation of a church-controlled organization at such a time weakened the Indian movement that had been developing strength and set the stage for denominational quarrels. No one really could have expected much else from such a move.

About the same time the Indian Affairs Branch initiated a number of steps that further weakened the organizational growth budding in Indian communities.

From the beginning the heavy expenses incurred by travelling Indian delegates to organizational meetings had been a major problem. In some cases, reserve communities were able to sponsor their representatives at least partially with proceeds from small bingos or dances. Regulations from the Indian Affairs Branch now were invoked forbidding the use of band funds or monies belonging to a reserve as contributions to Indian organizations. Even today, such contributions are limited to twenty-five cents per capita. In order to use their own money to further the work of their own organizations the Indian leaders had to go to the agent on their reserve, present their case and ask him for money for delegates to attend conferences. Usually the answer was: "The matter will be given consideration." And, naturally, that was the end of it.

Since the organizations functioned on a voluntary basis, without any offices or financial base, the members were expected to attend the annual meetings at their own expense and to bring to those meetings the resolutions from their respective communities. Toward the middle and latter part of the 1950s, the Indian Affairs Branch initiated a series of conferences supposedly aimed at determining the needs of the Indian people. In the province of Alberta, these meetings initially were called agricultural conferences. The reserve communities were supposed to talk about their agricultural needs and to be informed of resources available for the development of their agricultural potential. Since these were official, department-sponsored meetings, the expenses of the delegates were picked up by the branch. For the first time a per diem allowance was paid the delegates. These so-called agricultural conferences covered every conceivable topic except, possibly, agriculture and thus directly affected the strength of the Indian organizations within the provinces. Gradually the government added to the agenda of these conferences, changing their titles to meet their expanded purposes. They became economic development conferences and community development conferences and, eventually, all-chiefs' conferences. Each conference hurt the real Indian organization conferences, because most of the key members of a reserve usually chose to attend the one where all expenses were paid.

In the mid-sixties the government tried another tack. It organized provincial and national Indian advisory councils. Supposedly these councils were to advise the federal government on matters pertaining to Indians. However, the government's idea of consultation was to present to the advisory council, as a fait accompli, whatever scheme it proposed to try on the Indians next. Using its most silver-tongued speakers the Indian Affairs Department would do its best to persuade those Indians on the council that the scheme actually had been created by them. Indians elected or appointed to the advisory councils were in a very difficult position. The department informed them that they were assembled as individuals to advise the government on the feasibility of plans drawn up by the government for the Indians, but that they must keep in mind that their advice could be accepted or rejected, at the department's discretion. The government went to considerable pains to stress to the council members that they were present only as consultants and that they should not take it upon themselves to act as representatives or spokesmen for their people. Their expenses were paid for going to meetings convened by the department, but no money was provided at all for them to travel on their own reserve or on reserves in their area. They were not paid one cent to circulate among their own people and find out what was wanted or needed or how the various schemes advanced by the government might be received. These advisory members were not able to report anything to their own people on the reserves because, as the government quickly pointed out, they were not representing anyone and, moreover, they had no money for the necessary travelling. At the same time, the federal government propaganda mills ground out releases telling Parliament and the Canadian public that they were consulting √ representatives of the Indian people on every move they made.

For the most part, when the terms of advisory councils came to an end in 1968, the Indian people themselves insisted they be dropped. All they accomplished, for all their government doubletalk, was the embarrassment of many sincere but deceived Indian workers.

Unwittingly, some private organizations also contributed to the decline of the Indian organizations during the period from the mid-fifties to the mid-sixties. For example, the Indian-Eskimo Association, a white citizens' group based in Toronto which was set up to give support to the Indian people and symbolize the concern of the non-Indian Canadian, gradually began to assume the role of spokesman for Indians rather than a supporting role. Members of that association became more of a hindrance than a help to the development of strong Indian organizations, a goal to which they were committed, because they were acquiring funds sorely needed by the Indian groups from the two sources open to our people, the private sector and the public, that is, the government.

Curiously enough, another dissipating factor at this time was the Pearson government's war-on-poverty programme. This should have helped Indian people, and there was a surge of hope that it might. But the government chose a method known as community development as its vehicle to carry to Indian homes the needed aid. Under community development, workers went to Indian reserves and communities expressly to stimulate and motivate the Indians to help themselves. When the Indian Affairs Department discovered to its horror that the Indians were ready and eager to go forward on just that basis, they quickly hopped off the community development bandwagon. Carried to its proper conclusion, the programme very soon would have made the jobs of the government workers unnecessary. That was not a community development department officials were anxious to promote.

At the same time and as part of the war on poverty, a peculiar group called the Company of Young Canadians was formed. While the CYC was not created to serve any particular ethnic group in Canada, a large part of its programme soon was aimed at native communities. These young, instant experts on things Indian were, like community development officers, supposed to motivate the people to use their own initiative. Instead, bumbling and stumbling through community after community with little or no sensitivity to the feelings of the people they were going to help if it killed them, these dedicated amateurs discouraged and weakened Indian organizations. Some of them wanted to run the whole show, didn't want the Indians to progress except under their guiding hand. Some gave the curious impression they had invented the Indian. Nearly all were hopelessly unprepared for their tasks. The net result of their eager (and quite truly most of these young people meant well) fumbling was to weaken the base through which the Indian could express his needs and through which he had the best opportunity to press his case.

Now many of the organizational troubles and problems of the past four decades have been recognized and overcome. Strong provincial leaders are emerging and behind them, strong provincial organizations. A National Indian Brotherhood has been set up by and for Indians, with an office in Ottawa from which we can present our case for the first time on a national basis. We need more leaders and we need more leadership training, but we are not worried. The land is full of bright, eager young Indians who are better educated than their fathers, more aware of the problems and more determined to push through their own solutions.

More and more we can be confident that our future will rest in qualified but brown hands and that no gentle old man will have to sit, hat in hand, all day in any office at the whim of a petty bureaucrat.

Quiet
Revolution ...

New Strength at a Late Hour

The creation in 1969 of the National Indian Brotherhood symbolizes the beginning of the end of the struggle by the Indians of Canada to achieve unity. Its founding marked a significant milestone, for in spite of the differences among Indians throughout the country and despite their centuries of isolation from each other, the Indians of Canada finally have succeeded in developing an organization through which they can talk with each other and through which they can negotiate from strength with the federal government.

The founding of the brotherhood fulfilled the dreams of many of the early leaders of our people who laboured so long without reward for such a body. It also ushered in a new era in Indian politics that offers many difficult challenges and dangers to the present Indian leadership.

The problems facing the brotherhood will grow and, unless it is able to propose successful alternatives and offer workable solutions, the prospect for a quiet revolution in the immediate years ahead will greatly diminish. For many, the brotherhood represents the final attempt by Indians to try to solve their problems within the context of the political system of our country. If it fails, and particularly if it is destroyed by the federal government, then the future holds very little hope for the Indian unless he attempts to solve his problems by taking the dangerous and explosive path travelled by the black militants of the United States.

Maybe this is what the government wants, so that it will have the legitimate excuse necessary to solve the so-called Indian problem any way it sees fit.

Problems don't just fade away. Unless faced up to squarely and solved, they multiply. The time any leader or group of leaders has in which to face up to and solve a problem decreases constantly. Oppressed peoples' awareness grows more quickly in the times in which we live, as does the knowledge that no one any more has to remain supine and take a beating, whether from another person, from some agency or from circumstances. Our people read newspapers; we listen to radio and we watch television. We have automobiles and can be in a traffic jam in the city as quickly as many suburbanites. In spite of the extreme tardiness of our education, we no longer are isolated, not as a people. Perhaps not to quite the extent the urbanite is but, nonetheless, just as surely, we are part of Marshall McLuhan's global village. We can push a button and turn a dial on our television sets and be only seconds away from the landing on the moon.

We can and we have watched black riots in the United States and we can and we have pondered their lessons. Today's communications systems bring us, just as they bring you, an awareness of the struggles other people in other lands face, some worse than ours, some not as hopeless. Our people have seen the methods used by other groups in similar situations, and we have measured their successes—and failures. We are learning from others about the forces that can be assembled in a democratic society to protect oppressed minorities. These things, too, are our classrooms now and our textbooks. And we are learning our lessons well.

Our younger generation has become a majority in our society. The expectations of the new generation of Indians are more intense than those of their elders. Any lack of change in the status quo to them is intolerable. Our situation today is, in fact, critical because the younger generation has less patience than the older. It is later than most non-Indians understand.

As a people we are going through the third stage of a turnover in modern leadership. Right after World War II, the new generation of leadership that began to assert itself and continued to lead until the mid-sixties came from the ranks of the middle generation, a generation that was not under the influence of the traditional leadership of the elders but was, at the same time, hardly to be classed as radical. Those leaders were what you might call marginal Indians. They were a generation with one foot in the white world and one in the Indian world. They had spent their youth in the days preceding the war. The postwar period had given them at least a limited opportunity to receive further education.

They were concerned and interested in organization but they were uncertain of the path to take. To some of the highly critical younger generation it seemed they were too much the captives of the mandarins. The younger generation called them Four-Day Indians because they spent so much of their time in four-day conferences. Their critics weren't sure whether they were Indians all the time or just during such conferences. Sometimes they seemed more white or at least more subservient to whites than they were red.

They held power during the period of decline for the Indian organizations that took place in the mid-fifties and early sixties. In the early sixties those leaders were in the forefront of an effort to establish a national Indian movement which would represent both status and non-status Indians. They set up a National Indian Council (which had nothing to do with the government-promoted National Advisory Council) through which it was hoped all Indians would be able to present their views to the government. The creation of this organization really signalled the takeover from the elders by the new interim leadership.

This marked the first real attempt to break down regional and tribal barriers between native people which had been so encouraged by the federal government. The task was monumental. The leaders of the National Indian Council had no financial resources with which to build an organization with strong grass-roots support. The initial excitement and hope inspired by the creation of the council quickly subsided.

Many factors contributed to its failure. The deep division between registered and nonregistered Indians could not be bridged. The Métis or nonstatus Indians also were in the process of attempting to organize. However, their problems and consequently their aims were markedly different from those of the registered Indians. Provincial governments held power over the Métis. The federal government ruled the status Indian. Treaty Indians feared association with the Métis would jeopardize their relationship with the federal government and, more importantly, endanger their treaty or aboriginal rights. Priorities of the two groups differed greatly. Consequently, an attempt to build a national organization embracing both faced grave problems from the start.

Another negative factor was the inability of the older generation of Indians to understand the new leaders and what they were trying to do. The elders simply lived in a different world. The communication gap was too great for bridging. So the new leaders had to jog along without the support of some of the most influential of our people at the reserve level.

A third factor that proved impossible to overcome lay in another division within Indian ranks. The new National Indian Council never could establish a solid, representational base. The membership and the leadership of the council was constituted to a high degree by the urban and marginal Indian population.

The leadership came from those Indians who had moved to cities and, in many cases, were employed by the government. The reserve or rural communities were suspicious. Indian organizations which were based on the reserve communities were cautions about involvement with the National Indian Council and eventually that suspicion proved a fatal weakness. The intention had been the creation of a representative national movement, but its failure to attract the rural Indians gave the government the opportunity (which it seized with obvious relish) to question the representational base of the council.

In spite of its failure, the development of the council had signalled the start of a new day in Indian politics in Canada. Its rise and fall had demonstrated in a practical, concrete way the evolutionary path of Indian politics. The experiment had demonstrated to Indians in Canada what was workable and what ideals could not be attained in this manner. Before its demise in 1968, the council itself encouraged the creation of two national bodies to serve the separate interests of registered and nonregistered Indians. Study of the mistakes made by the council has given present leaders valuable insight into the pitfalls involved in trying to make a national organization work. The new national body benefits from the need shown by the old for recognition of the hard realities of Indian politics.

While many may claim that the National Indian Council was a failure, it was, nevertheless, an important and necessary first step from which a viable organization could grow. Like the early failures in the American space programme, these failures constituted a hard but important lesson. They were the prelude to Indian attempts to organize a body which would help solve some of our major social and economic problems.

In late 1967, leaders from all regions of Canada met in Toronto to dissolve the National Indian Council. Following the dissolution two separate organizations were created. One was to serve the Métis or the nonregistered Indian; the other was to work for the treaty and registered Indians of the country. The National Indian Brotherhood, created to serve the treaty Indian, was launched in a different manner than its predecessors. Discussions had been started among Indian leaders earlier that same year for the purpose of determining what type of structure would best serve the diverse needs of Indian peoples across the country. Through a continuing period of two years and after long and detailed discussions, the structure of the brotherhood took shape.

To serve widely varying needs of Indians all across the nation, the power and decision-making process was kept in the hands of the existing provincial organizations. The membership of the organization is based on its provincial affiliates rather than on the concept of individual membership. The provincial organizations appoint delegates to the national meeting, and it is these representatives who form the National Indian Brotherhood.

Representation is based on a formula of five thousand people or a portion thereof, thus giving proportionate representation to Indians in every part of the land. The national body cannot act on matters of provincial or territorial concern unless it has expressly been invited to do so by the member organization concerned. The national body can take the initiative, however, on issues that have national scope. Executive members are elected for two-year terms with the various regions electing their own representatives. The chief, or president, is elected by the General Assembly for a two-year term; if, during the course of his tenure, he should lose the confidence of two-thirds of the member organizations, he could be deposed by a vote of nonconfidence.

The underlying concept of the National Indian Brotherhood is that a broad national structure should exist in order to serve the member organizations rather than having the provincial or territorial members responsible or answerable to the national body. The people to whom the national leaders are responsible are the board and executive members of the provincial organizations who in turn are responsible to their members. Consequently, the national body can be only as strong as the provincial organizations which support it.

The structure of the national body was officially accepted at the founding meeting in Winnipeg, in July 1969. Present at the founding convention were representatives from all ten provinces plus the Yukon and the Northwest Territories.

Indian leaders know that the brotherhood's path will not be easy. Its continuing challenge and responsibility will be to adapt to the new leadership that is springing up in all parts of the country and to try to meet with justice and equity the diverse needs of our people living in all geographic areas of the country and in myriad social and economic circumstances.

Obviously its first challenge is survival itself. Officials of the federal government already have used the brotherhood's newness as an excuse for attempts to weaken the organization. They can be expected to bustle across the country hoping to divide our leaders and dilute any position taken by the brotherhood in opposition to federal government policy.

A key and immediate problem that must be overcome is the isolation of Indians from federal political leaders. To date, there has been little contact with the politicians of Ottawa. Such meetings as have been held with them have been short, giving no chance for extended discussion of problems or solutions. We realize that such leaders, the Ottawa politicians, generally speaking, are ignorant of the subject, understand the problems very dimly if at all. The advice they have gotten in the past has come almost totally from bureaucrats who know and understand even less, who have their own interests at heart rather than the interests of the Indian people. An immediate and major responsibility of the brotherhood is to open these channels of communication at every opportunity in order to clarify the real issues facing the Indians and to present Indian alternatives to such issues. We must, and soon, have our own representatives on hand in Ottawa to advise those who are genuinely concerned with our problems. With the brotherhood office now open in Ottawa, it is not enough that we offer information; this office must aggressively inform those politicians on any and every issue relevant to Indians.

Additionally, the Ottawa office of the brotherhood is responsible for seeing that a proper flow of information concerning plans and proposals the government may have or is developing for Indian people reaches the provincial organization offices across the country. The National Indian Brotherhood is not designed to be an organization imposing itself and its theories on the people it was created to serve. Its responsibility lies in the area of coordinating the activities of its members and ensuring that resources are made available to them so that they can fulfill the responsibilities they have for the people of their own areas.

Traditionally, the role of provincial organizations has been that of getting Indians together on a yearly basis to present their grievances to responsible officials and to draft resolutions to the appropriate levels of government for action. The government's role, presumably, was to take the necessary measures to solve the problems presented. Theoretically, this system ensured progress. In practice, the Indian leaders found themselves coming to meetings year after year to be faced with the same resolutions. The government happily sat back, letting the Indians go through the motions, doing absolutely nothing about the problems. The leaders of the Indian organizations were left with egg on their faces. Their own people sent them to these meetings to get a job done, to get problems solved. They were unable to follow through on their resolutions, because they had no money to hire personnel on a full-time basis. Most of the meetings they held were at their own expense as it was. The organizations faced continually the problem of trying to meet the growing needs of their people with an ever-diminishing supply of money and trained workers.

The changes over the past five years have posed difficult questions for our leaders. If the organizations are to remain viable as a means through which people can present their grievances for action, then the whole framework of the bodies must be altered. Each of the provincial organizations must establish offices and workers capable of helping local communities to define their problems but also ready and able to assist them in finding relevant solutions. Much work still can be done on a voluntary basis but the time for purely voluntary assistance has come to an end. Full-time, competent, trained and salaried workers must now carry the bulk of the workload in every office. The problems have increased to the point where the old haphazard, hope-to-get-the-work-done methods are obsolete.

This, of course, means money. Organizations in many cases recognized quickly the need for full-time offices and trained staff to set up the necessary administration. But pay them with what? Pine cones?

For every provincial organization, the first problem inevitably was where the money would come from. Ordinarily organizations are able to live and thrive on money received from their membership plus some portion coming from either the federal or provincial governments, perhaps some from a source or sources in the private sector. The Indian organizations could not expect their people to provide any great sums. If Indians have money they must buy food and clothing first. Obviously our organizations couldn't get funds from the federal government. Any request to Ottawa for money for an Indian organization would be turned over to the Department of Indian Affairs. Indians have known for a long time that any money from that source has strings attached in all sorts of unpredictable places. Even if, miracle of miracles, the department didn't try to control them on the basis of money granted, the leaders would be wide open to accusations that they were government bought, a fatal charge to any Indian leader. Until very recently, the provincial governments have stayed out of the picture, referring any hint of a request for help to Ottawa on the grounds that Indians are the responsibility of the federal government.

This leaves the private sector, always an area difficult for an Indian to appeal to with any hope of success. Many people are vocal in their sympathy for the Indian, but their sympathy seems to come to an abrupt halt if it means putting cash where their mouths are. Strange, for it seems to be easy enough for white people to gather money for their own pet projects on behalf of the Indians. Citizens' groups are particularly successful in gathering money from private sources, especially if they want to send teams of volunteers into Indian communities on some glorious self-help scheme. If white people want money, all they have to do is design an impressive-sounding research programme on Indians, present it to any level of government and, as if by magic, the money rolls in. The federal government apparently has no qualms about shelling out five or six million dollars for a company with a research programme aimed at Indians in northern Alberta, but it remains unwilling to give the Indians of Canada one-tenth that amount to do vital, long-needed research on their treaties and aboriginal rights, a research programme that would help solve the biggest problem separating the Indians and the government of Canada for the past hundred years.

Ottawa has refused to take a step that would aid Indian fund-raising efforts immensely. A major contributing factor in the success of fund-raising projects is tax-deductible status. Groups, individuals, companies and foundations are unwilling to give donations unless the group receiving the donation is on the tax-deductible list. Curiously enough, the Indian-Eskimo Association of Canada, a white citizens' organization dedicated to the native cause, had no trouble getting such status. But *Indian* organizations? No way.

Because white society is so ignorant of Indian advances, there remains an attitude that Indians cannot be trusted with large sums of money. Consequently, many donor sources feel they must give their money to white or white-dominated groups who will see to it that the money is not wasted by the savages. One wonders sometimes what would happen to all those dedicated white Indian sympathizers if the Indians went on strike for a year—just quit being Indian. Maybe the simplest answer would be for all Indian leaders in Indian organizations to declare themselves white. Then they could claim that they have some wonderful programmes for the poor benighted Indian and the money would materialize. Perhaps if the white society and its political leaders, although this is a lot to ask, were to use plain common sense about Indians, see them as human beings with man-made problems, then some progress could be made.

The prime minister makes a point of telling Indian leaders that solutions to the so-called Indian problem must be forthcoming from the Indians themselves. We couldn't agree more, but someone must be on the other end, listening to those solutions. Listen now, to one Indian leader talking about some of the desires of his people. "The land where I come from is good for farming, cattle ranching and other types of work. We are told by the government that we have to work. Here is a means by which we can work and earn our living, but we do not have the money or equipment that we need to clear our land or buy our cattle or pay salaries. Does the government expect us to farm our land with our fingernails?"

... or Red Explosion?

Cross-Purposes

The tough-minded resurgence of the Indian organizations has put more pressure on the federal government. Angry new Indian leadership has shocked the Canadian public by exposing sordid facts and situations that Canadians had myopically overlooked at their own doorstep. This, with the awakening interest of some non-Indian groups, has forced the government to stand up and account publicly for its mishandling of the native people.

For years, whenever the incredible Indian situation was brought to the attention of the public, the government countered with miles of statistics calculated to show how hard government officials were working and how many millions of tax dollars were going to help Indians. Miles of statistics were as sterile as they were stupid—clumsily redundant to anyone who had seen the reality of the situation on any reserve. However, for years it was easier for the public to believe comforting federal figures than to believe what its eyes could have seen, what its nose could have smelled and its heart should have rebelled against.

For example, no matter how the federal government quotes figures on the improving educational picture, the answer on any reserve lies with the alarming rate of students dropping out of school. If you are interested in studying the waste of human potential, talk to these dropouts. Ask them one question—why? Government apologists quickly point out that in 1960 there were around forty Indians in universities throughout Canada, a number which had risen to nearly two hundred by 1968. This is supposed to be an indication of the rate and record of improvement in education. The shame remains that there are far too few Indians in Canada with university education, and that the per capita enrollment is far, far below the proportionate rate of non-Indian Canadians in university.

The former minister of Indian Affairs, the Honourable Arthur Laing, may well be regarded as the most notoriously artful minister in the history of Canadian confederation for his efficient use of statistics to paper over the inadequacies of his department. For example, supposedly to meet the housing crisis which for decades had been plaguing Indians in Canada, he dramatically announced a one hundred and twelve million-dollar programme over a five-year period. After suitable fanfare and a well-publicized start, the time span was expanded quietly, without any publicity at all, so that the annual spending scarcely exceeded that of previous years. The impression carefully given to the Canadian people was that something important was happening to meet the housing needs of the Indians. The whole programme was wasted. The housing needs of the Indians are greater than ever today and even those houses built for one hundred and twelve million dollars during the Laing programme proved virtually useless to the people occupying them. They were never better than marginal slum dwellings and often proved worse—ill-conceived architecturally, unsound engineeringly and located disastrously. Nor was anything further done to meet the rapidly expanding needs for Indian housing.

Throughout his tenure as minister, Mr. Laing overworked his publicity department to convey the impression that he was labouring night and day to help solve the difficulties of the Indians. The clear inference was that Indians simply did not have the initiative to help themselves, and that it was because of Indian intransigence that Laing was unable to do a better job. The Honourable Mr. Laing's ignorance of the Indians in Canada in the mid-sixties was exceeded only by his arrogance. He had his foot in his mouth so often he surely must have learned to love shoe leather. His idea of a thoughtful solution was to tell Indians to get out and pull themselves up by their bootstraps. He never bothered to make sure they had bootstraps. His greatest contribution to the Indian situation came about because his silly doctrinal statements helped bring Indians from one coast to the other closer together.

During Laing's tenure, the power of the bureaucrats in his little empire grew steadily. Most of Laing's contacts with the Indians of Canada and most of his misinformation about them came from these autocratic mandarins. His ill-informed statements caused alarm and concern among Indian leaders across Canada and helped clear the vision of non-Indians who had begun to catch on to what was happening. After the election of Pierre Elliott Trudeau as leader of the Liberal party, than as prime minister of Canada, a new programme of government-native consultation was drawn up. These plans called for the minister to travel extensively to meet with Indians in every part of the country. Indian leaders shuddered at the thought of a dialogue with the Honourable Mr. Laing. Fortunately for all the Indians, the new prime minister called a June election, and the consultation meetings were delayed. Following the Liberal victory at the polls, Mr. Laing was given another portfolio and in his place two young members of Parliament assumed responsibility. Jean Chrétien became the minister of Indian Affairs and Northern Development, and Robert Andras, minister without portfolio responsible for the development of new objectives.

Indian leaders, briefly hopeful that Mr. Trudeau's Just Society might include native peoples, were ready to work with the new ministers. In a courageous speech in September 1968 in Toronto, Mr. Andras vowed that political leadership would supersede bureaucratic leadership. Unhappily for the Indians, the Andras promise was never fulfilled. Mr. Andras lost his round with the mandarins in Ottawa, and the Indians lost with him. The much-promised dialogue that was to develop through the so-called consultation programme proved to be, in the end, a fiasco that wasted the time of the Indian leaders. Meetings were held as promised, but they could never by any stretch of the imagination be called consultations, nor did they ever spark a dialogue. They did, however, provide the bureaucrats and their new mouthpiece, the Honourable Mr. Chrétien, the opportunity to say to Parliament and the Canadian public, "We consulted the Indians and as a result of those consultation meetings here is our new Indian policy."

If real consultation had taken place, if there had been a genuine dialogue or if they had even bothered to listen to what the Indians were saying during these preliminary meetings, the government would not have written a new policy paper or, when they did, their policy could not have ignored so completely the realities of the Indian situation.

Before the cross-Canada consultation meetings started, a pamphlet called *Choosing a Path* was mailed to all Indian families in Canada listing thirty-four questions that were to be answered. The questions dealt with the band council system, uses of land, education, the definition of Indians and things of that nature. They were worded in such a manner as to be answerable with a simple yes, no or maybe. Compilation of the answers supposedly would have provided the government with the information it needed to amend the *Indian Act*, that discriminatory piece of federal legislation that rules Indian life.

In July of 1968, with a great bash of publicity, the federal government opened its actual consultation meetings. Teams of bureaucrats poured out of Ottawa with either one of the ministers to actually meet and talk with real Indians, purportedly to find out which of the thirty-four questions received a yes answer, which a no answer and which ones the maybes. In short, the eyeball-to-eyeball meetings were supposed to give Indians a chance to say, "This is what we want; this is what we don't want; this is what we aren't sure about and would like to discuss further." From all the publicity put out about the meetings, the Indians had begun to believe the government really meant to talk with us and even to listen to us. We should have known that if the white man speaks with a forked tongue, the white man's public relations man speaks with a triple-tined tongue.

And the government surely had plenty of these triple-tined-tongue types around when the consultation programme got underway. The minister later stated that public relations firms had been hired to give publicity to the consultation meetings so as to expose the views of the Indian people to the Canadian public. It must have been a tough job for those publicity hirelings to make what the Indians had to say about government leaders sound good to the public. It makes more sense to think that the government had hired the publicity boys to beat the drums for them, not for us, to counter the terribly negative publicity the department had been receiving, to try to develop some sort of positive image for the Department of Indian Affairs. That seems like a really tough way to make a living.

The dialogue meetings began on schedule with the two novice ministers hitting the consultation trail like John Wayne and Gary Cooper to discover which path the Indians wanted to follow. For both Chrétien and Andras this was their first real exposure to Indian peoples. For them, it turned out to be the fork in the trail. Andras, not being tied down to a department, was able to get closer to the Indian people. He discovered quite soon on his trips that the things that occupied the minds of the Indians were not necessarily the areas covered by the thirty-four questions prepared under Arthur Laing. Indians everywhere made it obvious that they were interested in treaty rights, aboriginal rights and settlement of land claims first and foremost. Chrétien, perhaps because of his administrative responsibilities or perhaps because of his total dependence upon and faith in the mandarins of the Department of Indian Affairs, was taken in by the bureaucrats and received little real exposure to the Indians.

Indian leaders and their people had held real hope for a time that the consultation meetings would signify an about-face in treatment from the government and that a true dialogue could be started with the political leaders of the country. However, before too much time passed, Indians could see it was the same old story. Everywhere the bureaucrats were succeeding in blocking any genuine dialogue.

In Alberta and Manitoba, the Indian organizations requested time to prepare by consulting their own people at every level before the federal representatives held consultation meetings in the two provinces. The Indian Association of Alberta requested a six-month delay in order to give the organization time to meet people in every reserve and area so that the leaders might talk truly for their people. Except for noncommittal acknowledgments, no answer was given to this request until Andras arrived unexpectedly in Edmonton to meet with a group of leaders and to listen to their reasons for requesting the delay. Andras was accompanied by an assistant and by a bureaucrat named Churchman from the department. Andras asked that the association agree to the meetings as scheduled. He assured us the consultation meetings at this time were just preliminary get-togethers that had little importance beyond giving the Indian leaders and the ministers and government leaders a chance to get acquainted. He explained that more time would be given during a second round of consultation when the real business would be carried on. The Alberta Indian Association stuck by its position. Alberta leaders wanted to be fully prepared for the meetings and felt they could not truly represent their people and fulfill their obligations to them if they did not first make sure of their wishes. The minister offered a three-month delay instead of the six the Albertans asked. After Andras's return to Ottawa, the Indian Association of Alberta received a telegram informing it that three months had been granted. Instead of meeting in September, a December date was set.

Alberta leaders at once began preparing for the December meeting. Consultations were held in all areas of Alberta with all band council leaders. The government granted the Indian Association five thousand dollars to cover the cost of the travelling teams sent out to every reserve. The total cost came closer to twenty thousand, but this was covered by the bands themselves and by the voluntary assistance of many people.

The government had announced in the House of Commons, with a

great air of righteousness, that it was embarking on a policy of consultation with the Indians and that there would be no changes in relation to
the Indians until the consultation meetings were concluded. Suddenly,
in September 1968, the minister of Indian Affairs reversed his course
and made a surprise announcement that he was reorganizing his department. Even Mr. Andras was caught off base, for he, like Chrétien, had
solemnly pledged not once, not twice, but again and again that any
changes which took place in the department would come about only
through and after consultation with the Indian people. The announced
reorganization surprised and discouraged many Indian leaders. Not only
did they feel that faith had once again been broken, but they suspected
that the changes were in line with changes the government was planning in the *Indian Act*.

To the dismayed Indians a mockery was made of the consultation
meetings which already had started. These meetings were supposed to
be preliminary sessions at which the Indian people and the government
would discuss possible changes to come. Suddenly, changes affecting all
Indians were imposed. In retrospect, it is clear that the reorganization of
the department implemented in September 1968 was directly related to
the aims set out in the federal white paper of June 1969. The inescapable
conclusion is that the formulation of that policy came long before any
results could be expected from the phoney consultation meetings. The
meetings thus stand exposed as the purest hypocrisy.

In the course of their preparation for the consultation meetings, the
leaders of the Indian Association of Alberta recognized that they would
need the expert guidance of resource people in many areas of Indian life,
in the legal field, in education, in economic and social development, in
community planning, in nearly every aspect of life.

Lawyers would be needed to explain the legal terminology of the
Indian Act and, of course, to help frame properly various changes in legislation that would reflect the needs of the Indians. The question of education posed some difficult problems. The traditional means of education
had failed to meet the needs of the people. In order for the Indians to
benefit from existing educational facilities, new methods would have to
be examined. Obviously the assistance of top-level educators, experts
who could facilitate the presentation of realistic alternatives and who
would be able to fit such new approaches into the educational system of
the province, was essential.

The leaders of the association recognized the need for consultants in the field of economic development. Philosophical theories may be intellectual exercise, but what was needed was practical advice, such as how to get our hands on the money we needed for economic advance.

We needed guidance in all areas. Consultants were necessary to outline and define the physical resources available to the reserves, to suggest means of development and to advise as to how our communities could be tied more beneficially to the surrounding economy. We recognized the need for experts to help our people realistically draft the course of our future. Our social structures needed examination and overhaul to fit the different types of communities included in our provincial society. Leadership structures in the various communities needed reassessment to make certain they complied with the administrative legislation of the *Indian Act*. Even while the consultation meetings between the government and our people were going on, officials of the Department of Indian Affairs were developing and implementing changed forms of what they called local government. They obviously had preconceived notions of how the *Indian Act* would be changed in order to fit their new theories of local government. This was another indication of the hypocrisy of the government's position.

Both Alberta and Manitoba Indian organizations sought such top-level counsel. Both organizations realized that financial assistance was necessary to pay for high-quality guidance. Both organizations made requests to the federal government for money for such consultants. Both explained the need and the reasoning behind the need. Indian Affairs departmental officials maintained that such consultants were not necessary since the meetings were to be of a preliminary nature. The attitude of Mr. Robert Battle, an assistant deputy minister, was typically astonishing. To our specific request for legal counsel, he offered first a typical bureaucratic answer—no money was available since none had been budgeted for such a purpose. To this he added blandly that lawyers were not needed anyhow, since the consultation meetings did not pertain to any legal matters and that legal assistance was not necessary to answer the thirty-four *Choosing a Path* questions. If Mr. Battle does not consider the *Indian Act* a legal matter, I would like to know what his definition of law is. In any case, if the poor fellow is not aware that the *Indian Act* is a legal document, I find it difficult to understand how he ever managed to become an assistant deputy minister in the Department of Indian Affairs. The Indian organizations got the same bureaucratic runaround from the deputy minister, John A. MacDonald.

Consequently, the Indian people were forced to go into the consultation meetings without proper resources with which to make their case. They entered the meetings with repeated assurances from the ministers that the first round was a preliminary get-together mainly designed to enable them to get acquainted with the ministers from Ottawa and to enter into exploratory discussions. It was understood by the Indian people that a national meeting would be convened, where the preliminary results of the regional meetings could be assessed, and after that, a second round of dialogues would get into the gut problems.

In December 1968 regional consultation meetings were held in Edmonton and in Winnipeg. At both meetings Indian leaders, in complete agreement, made it crystal clear to federal government representatives that before any new working relationship could be established with the Indians, the outstanding questions of the treaty and aboriginal rights of the Indians would have to be settled. The government was told that on such a basis and only from such a base could work be started to solve the many pressing social and economic problems confronting Indians. The government was told in no uncertain terms that any discussion of changes in the *Indian Act* would not be considered until the question of treaty rights and aboriginal claims had been settled.

To Edmonton the government had the audacity to send a group of junior departmental officials, who had no more authority than the local regional bureaucrats, to meet with our top chiefs and leaders and spokesmen carefully assembled from all the reserves in the province. We refused to meet such underlings and the session was delayed until Ottawa dispatched Mr. Andras to Edmonton. We felt that if we were not to meet with our peers, there was no point in meeting at all.

The national consultation meetings which followed were convened in Ottawa in April of 1969. Once again federal bureaucrats showed unmistakably what little importance they really attached to our meetings. They had the gall arbitrarily to set the delegate number from each of the provinces without bothering to ask the respective leaders for their opinions as to a proper representational formula. The truth was obvious. They didn't care what we thought.

At the five-day conference, our leaders across Canada agreed that the Indians of Canada would not discuss the administrative framework as set out in the *Indian Act* until the question of Indian rights in general had been settled satisfactorily. Indian leaders unanimously agreed that a general declaration of intent containing the principles and spirit of the treaties and aboriginal rights would have to be adopted before any move by the federal government in the direction of new Indian legislation could be considered. Consequently, no discussion took place at that conference about changes in the *Indian Act*. The entire Indian assembly once more made it clear to the government: "Settle our rights, then talk legislation."

A National Indian Committee was formed to research and document the case for Indian rights. A cost estimate was drawn up and presented to the government. Our position was that, since the government had consistently refused to recognize its obligations, only proper research would provide the Indian people with the documentation necessary to reach an equitable settlement with the government. The government reluctantly agreed to put up the money requested for this vital research. After a summer of waffling came their September 16, 1969, announcement of operation and organization grants approaching three hundred thousand dollars, pathetically little compared to what was requested and *is required*. That is not good enough.

In spite of our repeated and documented efforts to make our position clear to the government, in the early summer of 1969 the minister proudly produced his infamous white paper, proposing entirely unacceptable plans for future government-Indian relations, plans that amount to total assimilation of the Indian, plans that spell cultural genocide. We could only assume, and it later was confirmed, that the author of the Just Society, Prime Minister Pierre Elliott Trudeau himself, approved of this travesty of justice.

If the government does not intend to honour its earliest and most sacred obligations to the Indian people, if the government has no concern for the integrity of its word, then the Indian people do not know how to deal with such people, and the Indian people will not deal with them. Indians know that nothing can be built upon the quicksand of deception.

If it is not now clear to the honourable minister, Mr. Chrétien, and to his deputy minister, Mr. MacDonald, that we will not talk with the government until the question of our rights is settled, then only God knows how to communicate with them, and if He does know how, surely He would have told them by now that they had not understood us.

Legislative and Constitutional Treachery

The MacDonald-Chrétien Doctrine

Despite the impression deliberately fostered by the government all during 1968 and early in 1969 that the meetings between Indians and the government were only of a preliminary nature, the federal government decided in June of 1969 to publish an Indian policy paper. Even to publish such a policy paper ran absolutely counter to everything the government had been telling the Indian people for a year and a half. The fact that the government stood ready to countenance such a hypocritical reversal of its word gives the lie to all the pious Ottawa utterances of the so-called consultation period. To make matters worse, however, it is quite obvious that during the exact period in which the government was theoretically pursuing consultation, federal officials, in isolation from the people they were supposed to be consulting, were plotting unilaterally a policy paper designed to alter the future of every Indian in Canada.

If one studies two major events that took place during the consultation process, one can understand why the federal officials were so anxious to downgrade the importance of the Indian-government talks. Even casual study illustrates the utter, barefaced hypocrisy of the department.

First came the reorganization of the Department of Indian Affairs and Northern Development in the fall of 1968. The official explanation of this move given in the House of Commons was that the reorganization was merely internal government business, hence no consultation with Indians was necessary.

Following a public airing of disagreement between the ministers (Chrétien and Andras) on that point, Mr. Chrétien hopped across the country meeting with Indian leaders to explain that one of the reasons for the reorganization was to upgrade services to the Indians. Competition between the officials of the two branches, Indian Affairs and Northern Development, was to accomplish this. Chrétien's other stated reason for his quick cross-country tour was to get acquainted with Indian leaders whom he had not had the opportunity to meet previously. These meetings were held privately. No members of the press were present, nor were the usual flocks of government flacks in evidence.

We have our own explanation of the reason for the sudden reorganization of the department. We know that originally the reorganization plan had been prepared under Mr. Laing and was in the final stages of plotting when he was transferred to a lesser portfolio. We know that the authors of the changes completed their plans during the change of ministers. We know that the new minister, Mr. Chrétien, came to his new responsibilities with little background in the problems of Indians or the machinations of Indian Affairs. The unvarnished truth is that the new minister knew little of his new duties and was forced to rely upon the goodwill and faith of his civil servant underlings. So, without adequate knowledge of the situation but with faith in the civil service bureaucracy, it appears that Mr. Chrétien signed whatever was thrust before him. Without really understanding what he was doing, he okayed the reorganization plan and then had to go along with it. Small wonder that such a reorganization of the department he was attached to caught Mr. Andras by surprise. It caught Mr. Chrétien by surprise, too.

The handwriting was on the wall for Mr. Andras, anyhow. Very early in his capacity as minister without portfolio within the Department of Indian Affairs, he had made it plain that he would not be responsible to nor would he be responsible for the actions of the mandarins within the department. He was already in the process of being isolated by the bureaucrats, simply because they did not have control over him. He was not safe.

Reorganization of the department without even a pretense of consultation was bad enough, but far more reprehensible was the secret preparation of policy to determine our future at the same time responsible officials supposedly were consulting our people on that very subject. The underhanded preparation of the document now established as Indian policy is a story in itself, for it was a case of continued struggle between department officials, headed by Deputy Minister John A. MacDonald, and the liberalizing forces led by Mr. Andras. Andras lost or, at least, was forced to compromise. The real losers, without even a chance to compromise, were the Indians of Canada.

The Indian leaders had been told that the consultation process was in its early stages and in such a context was not too important. That explanation was necessary to calm the fears of the Indians that they had not been given ample time properly to prepare for meetings billed as consultation on changes in the *Indian Act*. The Indians rightly feared that the department already had decided upon the course of action it would take. The Indians suspected that the department had two goals in pushing the meetings: to steamroller the unprepared Indians into accepting changes the department already had planned (and the sudden reorganization of the department didn't do much to dispel this fear), and to lull public opinion by leading the public to believe that the consultation meetings were genuine, and that the Indians actually were being heard.

The department hoped the public would be led to believe that any actions taken following the meeting would come about as a result of the consultation or indeed might be action requested by the Indians themselves. The department needed its image polished in order to get its programmes approved by the cabinet and at the same time effectively to neutralize embarrassing questions raised by members of the opposition in the House.

Given the fact that the government planners had seen to it that the Indians lacked time and resources effectively to prepare for the meetings or to outline their own course for the future, it would be quite normal for disagreement among the Indians to occur. If this happened, as seemed likely, the department could then tell Parliament and the country that no agreement could be reached among the Indians themselves. In such circumstances, the government would stand ready to present the changes it had already prepared, claiming that only these alternatives had received some sort of consensus.

Fortunately, although the Indian leaders were not as well prepared as they would have preferred, neither were they as badly fooled as the government would have liked. The division among Indians that had been foreseen by crafty government planners did not materialize. At the national consultation meeting in Ottawa in April 1969, Indian representatives concluded the session in unanimous agreement. Furthermore, to the chagrin of MacDonald and Chrétien, the Indians there refused to discuss the *Indian Act* at all. They knew that any discussion on changes in the act would give the bureaucrats a basis from which to draft their own changes, claiming, of course, that these had been requested.

Instead, the decision reached by the Indian leadership was that a national committee be created to coordinate a thorough investigation of Indian rights. Following the conclusion of such research, the government would be asked to settle equitably its legal and moral obligations to the Indians of Canada. Following such a satisfactory agreement and only after receiving such satisfaction, the Indian leaders would request and expect to help draft new legislation which would truly reflect the diverse needs of Indians across the country. Such an act naturally would have little similarity to the present legislation. Rather than presenting the Indian people with an unendurable fait accompli perpetrated by men both unaware and insensitive to the problems, such a new Indian act would place responsibility for their future squarely on the shoulders of the Indian people.

When the government drafted its new policy of inequality it became apparent that once again the white men had not heard us, they had not understood us, and one has to wonder if they even listened to us at the so-called consultation meetings. Some consultation!

In a way, when federal officials told us that the first round of consultation meetings were not important and were just preliminary, get-acquainted sessions, they were not lying. Those sessions really were not important. The Department of Indian Affairs and through it, the federal government, had already decided what it was going to do with and to the Indians of Canada. They knew, even if the misled Indians did not know that nothing would be changed because of our little talkfests.

We would be the last to deny that the white man makes beautiful talk. Take the following paragraph from the foreword of the new policy paper: "The Government does not wish to perpetuate policies which carry with them the seeds of disharmony and disunity, policies which prevent Canadians from fulfilling themselves and contributing to their society. It seeks a partnership to achieve a better goal. The partners in this search are the Indian people, the governments of the provinces, the Canadian community as a whole and the Government of Canada. As all partnerships do, this will require consultation, negotiation, give and take, and co-operation if it is to succeed."

This is a prime example of what we might call forked-tongue doubletalk. From bitter experience the Indian translates the last sentence of that paragraph.

For "this will require consultation," read: "We will come to tell you what we have decided for you, and it is in your best interest to agree."

For "negotiation," read: "Now that we have decided what is best for you, we want you to tell us which i's you want dotted and where you would like the commas."

For "give and take," read: "You give us what little you have left, and we'll take it all."

For "co-operation," read: "If you want the plans we have drawn up for you to succeed, you must work with us to implement them and in the process kill whatever helps to make you Indian, for we no longer think it wise for you to be Indian."

If the government actually meant any of their high-flown, forked-tongue rhetoric, then why has it not listened to Indian requests for the fulfillment, in modern terms, of the spirit and intent of the treaties? If the government even once had listened to us it couldn't have had the barefaced gall so openly to attempt to abrogate its legal and moral commitments and responsibilities.

The government's proposed new Indian policy is a curious and sick collage of empty clichés and distorted facts. It reflects only, but perfectly, the total lack of understanding possessed by its authors of the situation in which the Indians of Canada find themselves today. It bears a more than marked resemblance to the recent American policy of termination, which proved an utter failure. (That disastrous course of action was adopted in the early fifties under the Eisenhower administration, aimed at getting rid of Indian reservations and at the complete assimilation of American Indians. It was subsequently set aside as unworkable, but not until it had caused a great deal of suffering and deprivation.)

The Canadian Indian policy has no more chance of working but much more chance of creating additional problems. It shows a surprising lack of insight into the social situation faced by Canadian Indians and a remarkable confusion about the principle of rights and the nature of administrative legislation.

In its foreword, the policy states: "The Government believes that its policies must lead to the full, free and nondiscriminatory participation of the Indian people in Canadian society." Few would quarrel with such an admirable goal. The foreword goes on to say that "it [the government's goal] requires that the Indian people's role of dependence be replaced by a role of equal status, opportunity and responsibility, a role they can share with all other Canadians." The intention of the government may be good, but the realities of the situation are ignored. This particular sentence brings forth the first indication that the authors of this policy are unaware of the realities of life, not just in the Indian segment of Canadian society but in all modern society. Theoretically, of course, all Canadians have equal status, even Indians. Yet any fool can read government figures showing that one in five Canadians is poor enough to be in a state of dependency. According to the MacDonald-Chrétien doctrine, a magic wand in the shape of a government white paper is all that is needed to restore equality all round. The reality of hunger is difficult to ignore, however many white papers are waved at it.

The phrase *opportunity and responsibility* has a nice ring to it, but Indians have believed all this time that all Canadians already had opportunity and that all Canadians, even Indians, already had responsibilities. The use here of the word *responsibility* insultingly implies that Indians do not discharge their responsibility as citizens. In just one area of responsibility, taxation, there are very few Indians who do not pay some form of taxes faithfully, and I have never heard of any who maintain tax havens in the Caribbean. The policy prattles on about replacing the Indians' dependence with opportunity and responsibility but nowhere does it suggest the government fulfill its legal and moral responsibilities to the Indian.

The government proceeds to state: "The policies proposed recognize the simple reality that the separate legal status of Indians and the policies which have flowed from it have kept the Indian people apart from and behind other Canadians." The statement is a half-truth. The facts become totally distorted and false when this statement is related to the first point of the new policy which prescribes that the "legislative and constitutional bases of discrimination be removed." It is true that the *Indian Act* has been and continues to be a restrictive, repressive and discriminatory piece of legislation. It is true that the *Indian Act* is partially responsible for keeping Indians apart from and behind other Canadians. It is not true, however, to say that the treaty rights of Indians have had the same effect.

The inclusion of Indians in the Canadian constitution was made in light of the treaties that had been signed with the Indians by the crown, and in recognition by the crown that the concept of aboriginal rights existed. The first point of the policy statement confuses the administrative aspects (which the government consistently has mishandled) with the government's legal and moral responsibilities. The treaty rights and aboriginal rights, which the policy paper calls constitutional discrimination, are rights that the government of Canada, not the Indians, has yet to fulfill.

Anyone can point out that the *Indian Act* has been responsible for holding the Indians of Canada behind other Canadians. How many stop to ask what the origins of the legislation were and who the people responsible for it were? It wasn't the Indians. Theoretically, the *Indian Act* was created to implement Indian rights as outlined in their treaties with the crown. The Indian Affairs Department was set up to administer and fulfill the terms of the treaties. However, the authors of the Indian legislation were men who grew up in the imperialist, colonial era of the nineteenth century, and the act faithfully reflects their environment. The *Indian Act* never at any time reflected the spirit or the intent of the agreements between the Indians and the Canadian government. It was in fact cleverly devised to achieve an entirely different mission. The *Indian Act* reflected the needs and wishes of the federal officials and the hierarchy of various religious denominations, never those of the Indians. The rankest sort of religious discrimination was deliberately written into the act to forbid such ceremonies as the potlatch and the sundance, both of which had religious significance. Indians who participated in these ceremonies were subject to prosecution. The excuse for this was twofold: the department wanted to civilize the Indians as fast as possible and the continued practice of Indian ceremonies delayed their progress; church officials eagerly christianizing Indians feared the competition of even a hint of the Indians' pagan past.

The government has admitted that its legislation has been repressive, but it failed to put its finger on an even more repressive factor, the civil servants within the Department of Indian Affairs. These people have as much responsibility, if not more, for the fact that Indians have been kept apart from and have lagged behind other Canadians as does the legislation they created and administered. Perhaps the coincidence that department officials prepared the policy paper somehow prevented the government from recognizing and admitting that its civil servants bear a greater responsibility for the difficulties facing the Indian people in Canada than any legislation in the nation's history.

The policy paper aims initially to convince the Canadian people that legal and constitutional status together are the major reason Indians lack equality with other Canadians. For both, it uses the word *discrimination* to appeal to the social conscience of Canadians and to minimize argument against its argument. The first point goes entirely counter to the wishes of Indian peoples in Canada. Again, the Indian people had stated that they did not want to discuss any changes in the *Indian Act* until the government had settled the outstanding issues of treaties, aboriginal rights and claims. In attempting to remove all constitutional protection for Indians, the government is attempting to eliminate unilaterally, once and for all, its obligations under the treaties as understood by Indians. Its clever and diabolical reference to discrimination constitutes an attempt by the government to sneak through the thoroughly illegal and immoral abrogation of Indian rights. Canadians who are not aware of the legal and moral implications of the government's policy are put in the difficult position of appearing to argue for discrimination if they oppose the government position.

The government attempts to argue, quite falsely, that the poverty of Indians as an ethnic group is caused by their legal and constitutional status and that if only they would become Canadians instead of Indians their poverty would magically end. One needs only examine the position of the nonregistered Indians or Métis to find that their precious supposed constitutional and legal equality has failed, almost criminally, to mean equality socially, economically or even legally.

Another interesting and revealing sentence in the foreword reads: "Indian people must be persuaded, must persuade themselves, that this path will lead them to a fuller and richer life." Keep this particular statement in mind in light of what the policy paper proceeds to say on the next page and in view of the infamous pamphlet that was circulated among Indians across the country prior to the so-called consultation meetings.

In its summary the government white paper said, among other things: "The review has drawn on extensive consultations with the Indian people, and on the knowledge and experience of many people both in and out of government. This review was a response to things said by the Indian people at the consultation meetings which began a year ago and culminated in a meeting in Ottawa in April. This review has shown that this is the right time to change long-standing policies. The Indian people have shown their determination that present conditions shall not persist."

If the policy paper was written in response to things said by Indian people or in consultation with them, then why is persuasion necessary to get Indian assent to the white paper? Consultation implies some understanding had occurred between the parties concerned. None did. Response implies reaction to another's act. There was no Indian action toward obtaining new legislation at this time. Exactly the opposite was true. If the policy paper depended upon Indian response to the questions in *Choosing a Path*, then the government must have answered the questions for the Indians. That pamphlet was never discussed at the national consultation meetings. In spite of all that the government can say, the truth is that the government never truly consulted the Indian people while this new policy was being drafted. The government knew damned well that its proposals would meet strong opposition and obviously has concluded that any means necessary to persuade Indians to accept a future made in Ottawa by civil servants for civil servants would be utilized.

Prior to 1969 it was nearly impossible to drag a minister out of Ottawa to meet with Indians. Since the publishing of the white paper, it has been difficult to get Indians together without Jean Chrétien showing up. The minister has indicated a flexibility and desire, as remarkable as it is sudden, to meet with Indians, Indians and more Indians. In the face of this, some provincial organizations have plainly but politely told the minister they prefer a period of time to draft a counterpolicy paper —a red paper, if you will—and until such time as they are ready for him, he should go somewhere else, anywhere else. Indians reason that the government knows its policy has been rejected and see no reason to pull a man as busy as the minister surely must be out of Ottawa to some reserve just to tell him something he already knows. We like to believe the red man can be as thoughtful as the white man.

We are not against any meeting that might serve a useful purpose, but before such meetings can occur, we must have time to write our own policy paper, one that will place our alternatives before the government and the people of Canada.

It would be tempting to interpret this phenomenon of the travelling minister as indicative of a new era of Indian-government relations that could lead to harmony and goodwill, if only we could erase from our memories experiences of the past—and some of the past is as recent as yesterday. One of the tactics frequently used by Indian Affairs officials to neutralize any opposition to current policy has been the contrived meeting with government Indians. (Government Indians are the equivalent of Uncle Tomahawks, Indians who place a higher value on their jobs than their heritage, Indians whose work for the government has compromised them.) Following such a meeting, the federal officials announce that they have met and consulted with a representative body of Indians, and the Indians have approved what the department is doing. Or they may make it seem more realistic by saying that only a minority disagree with whatever the proposal may be. Another variation is to say that they have found such disagreement among the Indians that they don't know what else to do.

The Indian people, especially their leaders, have become all too familiar with the divide-and-conquer ploys of the department. It is because of decades of unfortunate experience with the department, experiences seemingly always ready for instant replay, that Indian leaders view the sudden interest of Mr. Chrétien with concern, misgivings and downright scepticism.

In spite of the fact that their new policy proposals have been flatly rejected by the people most concerned, the Indians, and by the people next concerned, the provincial governments, the department keeps on trying. Information reaching Indian leaders indicates that the government is pressuring white organizations such as the Indian-Eskimo Association to persuade Indians that the federal white paper is the right path for Indians to walk and that they must accept it. Prime Minister Trudeau has publicly, on several occasions, told Indians in various parts of the country that the government does not intend to honour its treaties, and that the new policy is the only path open to the Indians. And the minister's frenzied reserve-hopping continues to point toward one objective, selling the white paper. Under the wonderfully appropriate headline, "Soft-sell plan adopted on new Indian policy," Ben Tierney of Southam News Services reported that, three months after the policy statement, the department was "[avoiding] talk of a five-year deadline for the policy's implementation. Instead, they [are talking] of a process of gradualism, implementing the policy whenever and wherever they can.... The idea is to dampen down the highly volatile atmosphere of confrontation that has developed since the new policy was announced.... [The department] will await the advent of a less emotional atmosphere" (*Edmonton Journal*, 17 September 1969).

The Indians of Canada do not employ public relations men to translate their dreams into commercially attractive goods. We will be on our guard against the department's gradual usurpation of our leaders' new strength, whenever and wherever it appears. We will not be dampened down, nor will we await the advent of relaxed public awareness, an atmosphere that would allow the government to proceed quietly with its unilateral abrogation of our rights.

The supposed new policy is no different than the arbitrary dictations from Ottawa to the Indians that have been repeated down through our history. Superficially, the government white paper is wrapped in nice middle-class platitudes that reveal, upon examination, no content, no meaning. In spite of all government attempts to convince Indians to accept the white paper, their efforts will fail, because Indians understand that the path outlined by the Department of Indian Affairs through its mouthpiece, the Honourable Mr. Chrétien, leads directly to cultural genocide. We will not walk this path.

Points One,
Two and Three

Hollow Commitment

Throughout the MacDonald-Chrétien white paper, which proposes to determine the future of all Canadian Indians, one vital element is missing. The role of the Indian has been totally overlooked. In sections where nominal obeisance is made to the Indian, he is allotted the role of a puppet that does only what is wanted of him, never what he wants. The attitude of the federal government screams at the Indian, "Yours is not to reason why but to do as I bid."

The Indian policy paper contains six major points, accompanied by five proposed steps that would create the framework for the Indian future.

Point one of the government white paper states that the government believes "the legislative and constitutional bases of discrimination must be removed." The government proposes to repeal the *Indian Act* and suggests that "enactment of transitional legislation to ensure the orderly management of Indian land would do much to mitigate the problem." Indian leaders repeatedly have informed the government that they do not want the *Indian Act* repealed until the government settles the outstanding issue between it and the Indian people—the question of Indian rights.

We do not want the *Indian Act* retained because it is a good piece of legislation. It isn't. It is discriminatory from start to finish. But it is a lever in our hands and an embarrassment to the government, as it should be. No just society and no society with even pretensions to being just can long tolerate such a piece of legislation, but we would rather continue to live in bondage under the inequitable *Indian Act* than surrender our sacred rights. Any time the government wants to honour its obligations to us we are more than ready to help devise new Indian legislation.

Meanwhile, the untimely suggestion for the creation of transitional legislation related to Indian lands can only create more suspicion. On the one hand, the federal government attempts to shove the Indian over to provincial jurisdiction, while on the other it proposes to keep its own fingers in the plummier parts of the pie. Ottawa would love to toss the political headaches to the provinces and at the same time make certain it still has some control over Indians, but without the consequences of its responsibility. The federal proposal to eliminate constitutional responsibilities, once and for all time, is totally unacceptable to the Indian people.

The prime minister or the minister of Indian Affairs can try all they want to use the emotional sacred cows of Canadian society as an excuse illegally to abrogate the rights of Indians. The fact remains that until they commit the Canadian government to honouring its legal and moral responsibilities, the cry for partnership with Indians will fall on deaf ears. The concept of partnership implies mutual trust and respect. In the area of treaty or Indian rights, no relationship of trust and respect exists. The prime minister and the minister can proclaim all they wish that there should be no treaties between segments of the same society, but that does not disguise nor alter the fact that such treaties do exist. Such contracts cannot be wiped out unilaterally because one side has milked the other and now wants to get out without fulfilling its side of the agreement. This is like the old story of the fox that lost its tail when it was frozen in the ice. The tailless fox then proposed to the other foxes that "we all cut our tails off since they are heavy and useless burdens." We do not propose to be tailless foxes for the government.

If Ottawa is serious about treating Indians the same as any other minority group in the country then it is incumbent upon the government to respect and honour the rights of Indians. The rights of other minority groups have never been taken away by the government. Corporations enter this country under special agreements. Those agreements are honoured. The French Canadian has his language rights protected by the Canadian constitution. This constitutes a treaty between segments of the same society. There is one big difference. The Québecois have Quebec and are politically powerful. Are we to understand that the concept of the Just Society then is based only on power, numbers and strength? If so, neither the Canadian Indian nor the average Canadian can expect real justice from their government. If the government truly opposes constitutional discrimination then it will, of course, remove all references to French Canadians or English Canadians from the Canadian constitution. Naturally, the newly passed languages bill must be revoked. In light of the government's own definition of equality and discrimination, it just isn't fair to either the French Canadian or the English Canadian that they should be discriminated against while the Indian thrives on a government-created environment of equality and nondiscrimination. The Canadian Indian wouldn't dream of asking for such an unfair, unequal advantage. Logical extension of the MacDonald-Chrétien doctrine makes it entirely unthinkable that the status of the French Canadian should be constitutionally enshrined. That would constitute a contractual agreement between two segments of the same society. Perish the thought that the French Canadian should be accorded special treatment as a member of a founding nation. The MacDonald-Chrétien policy asserts that all Canadians are the same.

The second point of the policy paper proposes that there be "positive recognition by everyone of the unique contribution by Indian culture to Canadian society." This is downright silly, the vaguest and most meaningless of the six points. How can matters of that sort be legislated? Anyone can, of course, pay lip service to a generality of this sort. The odd thing is that this point is supported by perfectly valid arguments that might well have been lifted bodily from any speech given by one of the increasing number of articulate Indians throughout the country. For example, the statement (in the policy paper): "It is important that Canadians recognize and give credit to the Indian contribution. It manifests itself in many ways; yet it goes largely unrecognized and unacknowledged. Without recognition by others it is not easy to be proud." A sound position, but of little immediate relevance. The statement is hollow because it fails to point any way in which such recognition will be accomplished. The point is expanded in the policy statement: "The principle of equality and all that goes with it demands that all of us recognize each other's cultural heritage as a source of personal strength." That statement would be welcomed by Indian people if it had any action behind it. The cultural heritage of Indians is ingrained in the historic question of Indian treaties and Indian rights. Without this basic recognition, the Indian cultural heritage can never be really appreciated by the non-Indian Canadian society.

Theoretically, of course, government officials and non-Indian Canadians are free to begin any time appreciating the Indian for what he is, as he is. The question is: how does this happen? Do you suppose that a large segment of white society, after carefully reading the policy statement, suddenly will discover and acknowledge that they actually love Indians? Maybe some of them will realize that some of their best friends are Indian. Others, perhaps not quite so sensitive or quick, may develop a new hobby of watching natives doing their quaint and picturesque dances. Surely they will find the regalia colourful and will go away feeling that it sure is good to have all that great old Indian culture around. A few may go so far as to invite an Indian to dinner, just as a tangible expression of their open-mindedness. Many can safely pay lip service by reciting the names of Indians they know, nice native boys who are not, of course, the kind you see downtown on skid row. It is doubtful that many will go as far as to permit their daughters to marry one, however.

The government proposes that the Department of the Secretary of State will support associations and groups to help Indians reach a greater appreciation of their cultural heritage. This is a friendly proposition of some merit, but it will become more believable when the government puts its money where its mouth is. More than that, we will want to know how much money will be spent this way, how it will be made available to Indian organizations, who will decide the terms of reference as to what constitutes the task of promoting greater appreciation of native heritage both within and outside the Indian society. Any approach to provincial governments for support to promote a positive Indian image must be initiated and carried out by the Indian groups or organizations involved. Keep in mind that no matter what efforts are made by the government to promote Indian culture, those efforts are doomed to failure unless it takes the initiative to recognize and accept the question of Indian rights. The government cannot expect members of society at large to respect Indians if it does not set the example.

Keep in mind, also, that no amount of preaching by the federal government about goodwill and acceptance of Indian values can change the attitude of Canadians generally unless the Indian achieves the position of economic self-sufficiency. In international politics, Chairman Mao states, power comes from the muzzle of a gun. In Canadian society, power comes from the crackle of the almighty dollar bill. Canadian society is materialistic. It is not long on humanist tendencies. As long as Canadians are expected by their government and led by their government to have pity and tolerance for the Indian, real acceptance will not be forthcoming. Respect does not flow from pity. The average Canadian respects and understands the message of the dollar. As long as the Indians do not have economic power, then they will remain subject to the pity of their fellow Canadians and the arrogance of governments which do not see any necessity to honour their obligations because the Indian is strong in neither dollars nor votes.

Point three of the government white paper proposes the transfer of Indians from federal responsibility to provincial jurisdiction. The paper directs that "services must come through the same channels and from the same government agencies for all Canadians." To implement point three, the federal government says it will propose to the governments of the provinces that they take over the same responsibility for Indians that they have for other citizens in their provinces. The take-over would be accompanied by the transfer to the provinces of federal funds normally provided for Indian programmes, augmented as may be necessary.

When an Indian looks at point three he can't help but wonder if those people in Ottawa are all on grass or something. What happened to their thinking powers? They appear unable to differentiate between way-out theory and the realities of life. Does the federal government really expect us to believe that by sloughing off its responsibilities onto the provincial governments, the social and economic problems of the native people will disappear? The theory of common services is all right, but the social, political and economic condition of the Indian is such that equal services simply will not meet the needs of our people. We aren't starting on equal grounds. Equality of services doesn't mean a thing to people who are so far behind they can't even see the starting line. It just means we would stay that far behind. That's not good enough. We want to catch up. Then we can talk about equality.

There cannot be any serious discussion regarding extension of provincial services to Indians until federal settlement is reached on the question of Indian rights. We have no treaties with provincial governments, but we do with the federal government, even if they are not honoured. A statement by the queen's first minister or by her government, that the question of treaties between the Indian and the government represents an anomaly, does not in any way constitute a settlement on the matter of Indian rights. In fact, it hardly constitutes a sensible approach. Certainly it does nothing to indicate the Trudeau government is willing to give serious consideration to the question of Indian rights. For the Indian this does not mean that the question has been answered or settled; it just means that there is some more extremely hard negotiation in store for him.

The plan of the federal government to begin negotiation immediately for extension of provincial services is premature. Even if agreements could be reached between the two levels of government, and there is no indication as yet that many provincial governments intend to accept the proposal, they will not receive any cooperation from Indians. To us those negotiations can only be viewed as political manoeuvres on the part of the senior government shamefully to rid itself of its obligations. There is no trust between the Indian and the federal government. If provincial governments interfere before such a basis of trust can be created, they will only encounter the same suspicion and mistrust the federal government has earned for itself over the years. The provincial governments cannot afford to be tarred with the same rotten brush and expect to establish the type of relationship necessary even to start tackling the many problems they would inherit.

The white paper states: "There can be no argument about the principle of common services. It is right." If the government was as vocal and self-righteous about its legal and moral obligations to the Indians of Canada as it is about its verbal dedication to the concept of equality, it wouldn't have to spend so much of its time and energy paying empty lip service to the latter idea. The authors of the policy paper overlooked two basic factors: the social and economic condition of Indians throughout the land and the role and responsibility of the Indians themselves in solving the problems they face.

The government policy paper says: "It is in the provincial sphere where social remedies are structured and applied, and the Indian people, by and large, have been non-participating members of the provincial society." Perhaps it is logical to assume that social problems should be solved at the provincial level. Perhaps the Indian is just a foolish red man to look at the condition of the poor people in every province and wonder what happened to the theoretical solutions that are supposed to exist at the provincial level. Perhaps the Indian is foolish to examine the plight of the Métis population. Those people have been receiving the benefit of provincial remedial structures for decades and a hell of a lot of them are even worse off than the treaty Indian. In fact, when an Indian looks at this segment of the native population, he is inclined to wonder what ever happened to the wonderful theory of equality or the even more wonderful theory of the Just Society.

The Province of Alberta is about the only provincial government in Canada seriously working at solving the problems faced by its Métis

citizens, but even Alberta has a long road to travel. In order even partially to alleviate some of the problems faced by the Métis, the provincial governments will have to expend enormous amounts of money,
amounts big enough greatly to strain and test their remedial structures.
This is not taking into consideration the added responsibilities of their
treaty Indian populations. If the provincial governments assume full
responsibility for their Indian populations, the expense and strain on
the budget will be astronomical. In each of the reserve communities, full
road systems have to be created; proper school facilities built, special
educational programmes started in order to tie the Indians into the economic structure of the province. The province would have to solve all
the problems the federal government has shirked for so long—housing
shortages, welfare programmes, health services. Many areas of social
development would have to be strengthened. If the provincial governments were to look seriously at the problems the federal government
wants to dump into their laps, they would recognize that their budgetary
considerations would be strained just meeting day-to-day needs let alone
financing all the special programmes that should be undertaken. And,
once again, no cooperation can be expected from the Indian people until
the question of their rights has been satisfactorily settled.

The authors of the white paper state: "Many services require a wide
range of facilities which cannot be duplicated by separate agencies.
Others must be integral to the complex systems of community and
regional life and cannot be matched on a small scale." Recently the
Indian has received some experience bearing on this question. Many
agencies have been popping up in regions where there is a large native
population. They receive their funds to do their thing for the area. The
agencies inform the native people that they are there for everyone, not
just the native people, although the constituency they serve usually runs
over seventy-five percent native. Their loudly professed aims prevent
the native people from protesting the imbalance of expenditures and
services and give the agency the unhindered control it seeks. For
camouflage, some native people may be hired to give the brownish tinge
that enables the agency to justify its existence to the outside world. So,
again we have reason to be suspicious of any theorizing about the inclusion of Indians in regional economic development. The experience of the
Indian has been and continues to be that when economic development
comes to an area where there are Indian communities, the economic
assistance goes first to all neighbouring non-Indian communities, and if

any is left over, it may or may not go to the Indian communities. Even natives living in white communities, especially in "moccasin flats" or in the ghetto sections of towns, do not benefit from any economic assistance given to the communities where they live. The one big benefit they do get is the increasing hordes of social workers who come prying into their lives, analysing their problems but never supplying the resources necessary to solve those problems.

In talking about programmes and services, the government proposes to negotiate with the provinces the amount of funds necessary above and beyond the present funds being expended. Tidily, the government explains that the proposed transfer of funds to the provincial governments and the scattering of responsibility to other federal departments theoretically would solve the so-called Indian problem. The third section of the white paper totally overlooks the expressed desire of the Indian to solve his own problems. In fact, where the Indian has had in the past to fight one bureaucratic monstrosity in order to accomplish anything, he will now be faced with ten or twenty bureaucracies, all boasting the same lack of understanding that the Department of Indian Affairs has so gloried in.

However, the proposal to scatter responsibility to other federal departments has both merits and drawbacks. The Indian has found that the more departments involved, the greater the tendency to play the old game known as passing the buck. And a lot of bucks are weary of the game. Another factor is the obvious intention of the Department of Indian Affairs to redeploy its forces. Deputy Minister MacDonald has announced to his empire of civil servants that a task force is being created to place civil servants currently employed by Indian Affairs in positions that will be opening in the various federal departments which will be assuming new responsibility for Indians and in the various positions that will be created by provincial governments as they assume jurisdiction. This obviously means that the same bunch of court jesters who have shown total inability to cope with their responsibilities in the department will be exercising their incompetency in key new areas. It is too much to expect them suddenly to acquire a bundle of common sense because they have turned up behind new desks. This fact alone is enough to guarantee failure of the government plan. For Indians it will mean that a bad situation will be worse, because we will have to battle those fools in ten or more bureaucracies instead of one.

It is difficult to understand why or how the federal government misjudged the current Indian situation so badly. Year after year through the past couple of decades, research project has piled on top of research project, all aimed at examining the plight of the Indian and recommending solutions. It seems obvious that the authors of the policy statement could not have done their homework properly. Even the latest major research project, the Hawthorn report, costing some quarter of a million dollars and filling two huge volumes, seems to have been relegated to dusty files somewhere in Ottawa.

For a new government that boasts it is attempting to lead the country in a new direction toward the creation of a just society, the federal white paper on Indians performs a huge disservice. The government insists upon being polite about Indians. Our problems are not polite ones. Is it that important to invent respectable analyses of our situation, when reality should be enough to move men to action? And are all the government's pretty, tidy predictions necessary? Isn't a future of cooperation with the Indian, of hard work leavened with trust and goodwill, good enough for them?

Points Four, Five and Six

Guilt Waived

The fourth, fifth and sixth points of the MacDonald-Chrétien doctrine deal with enriched services, claims and treaties and Indian lands.

Under the fourth point the policy states: "Those who are furthest behind must be helped most." Once again we have a reasonable theory but a number of unanswered questions. The paper says: "The Department of Regional Economic Expansion, the Department of Manpower and Immigration, and other federal departments involved would be prepared to evolve programmes that would help break past patterns of deprivation." The proposal offers little that is different from the past. Utopian programmes to meet the needs of Indians have always evolved from Ottawa. The question that has to be asked is how much difference plans drawn up by other departments will make, especially since we have seen that these other departments are going to be filled chock full of redeployed experts from Indian Affairs, the department which has been perpetuating patterns of deprivation all along.

The magic paper says: "In an atmosphere of greater freedom, those who are able to do so would be expected to help themselves, so more funds would be available to help those who really need it." Who would determine who is able to help himself? Who would play the role of the authority figure who expects people to help themselves? What body would determine the really needed assistance and, finally, what body would control the funds that are supposed to be available?

The MacDonald-Chrétien doctrine says: "The transfer of Indian lands to Indian control should enable many individuals and groups to move ahead on their own initiative." The arrogant assumptions of the policy paper in this instance become inexcusable, since no agreement has been reached in regard to the type of land control that would be assumed by the Indian either individually or collectively. In fact, discussion has not even begun.

The government white paper promises "to make substantial additional funds available for investment in the economic progress of the Indian people." Accompanying the presentation to the House of Commons, the Honourable Minister announced a fifty-million-dollar fund. Besides offering an incredibly inadequate fund, we wonder whether Mr. Chrétien is copying Mr. Laing's fiasco of the $112-million housing scheme. If so, the Honourable Minister should remember that Mr. Laing's announcements were considerably more impressive than his accomplishments. Is his only another case of labouring mightily to bring forth a mouse?

Dealing with the problem of overpopulation in reserve communities, the MacDonald-Chrétien doctrine notes: "Even if the resources of Indian reserves are fully utilized, however, they cannot all properly support their present Indian populations, much less the populations of the future." It continues: "Many Indians will, as they are now doing, seek employment elsewhere as a means of solving their economic problems." As a solution, it proposes: "Jobs are vital and the Government intends that the full counselling, occupational training and placement resources of the Department of Manpower and Immigration are used to further employment opportunities for Indians. The government will encourage private employers to provide opportunities for the Indian people."

The government's intentions are noble, but good intentions by themselves will not solve the employment difficulties that the Indian faces. Counselling people about jobs that do not exist will not alleviate the problem of unemployment. Training people for jobs that are not available wastes everyone's time and energy. Training people to be catskinners and mechanics may be fine, but some attempt should be made to determine how many catskinners or mechanics are going to be needed. It does no reserve any good to have the best crew of unemployed catskinners in the country. Too many of the present job-training programmes are wasteful, misdirected and do little to help the trainees. Thirty years ago a man would have been trained to use a shovel properly, or to do a good job of rootpicking, but it is about time the government discovered that the need for rootpickers has fallen off.

The unemployment training proposals of the white paper place the Indian who is interested in being a farmer in an unenviable position. On the one side, Mr. Chrétien and his brain trust provide the training to make him a good farmer and teach him to get the maximum production from his land. On the flip side, the prime minister tells all farmers to produce less since the government cannot sell their produce.

Concluding point four, the authors of the federal white paper advise the Indian that the Department of Regional Economic Expansion will meet his needs. Considering that this is a new department, there is a faint ray of hope that it may be more successful than its predecessors, but don't blame the Indian if he is sceptical and replies to the government, "Promises, promises, promises!"

The MacDonald-Chrétien doctrine reaches the peak of its glory, the epitome of arrogance, doubletalk and ignorance in its fifth section, entitled "Claims and Treaties." It sanctimoniously proclaims: "Lawful obligations must be recognized," and then devotes three columns of space affirming that as far as the government is concerned, it has little or no legal obligations. In a caustic, superior tone, in a manner which can only be interpreted as telling the dumb Indian that he doesn't know what he is talking about, the federal white paper asserts: "Many of the Indian people feel that successive governments have not dealt with them as fairly as they should. They believe that lands have been taken from them in an improper manner, or without adequate compensation, that their funds have been improperly administered, that their treaty rights have been breached." There isn't an Indian worth his buckskin jacket who wouldn't agree with that. The white paper continues sarcastically: "Many Indians look upon their treaties as the source of their rights to land, to hunting and fishing privileges and to other benefits. Some believe the treaties should be interpreted to encompass wider services and privileges, and many believe the treaties have not been honoured."

In an astounding abandonment of logic and common sense, the federal government then, in all its majesty, attempts airily to dismiss the treaties by saying: "Whether or not this is correct in some or many cases, the fact is the treaties affect only half of the Indians of Canada." Of all the deliberate, barefaced hypocrisies, this one wins the beaver tail. First it tries to tell us that simply because half of the Indians of Canada never signed treaties, those signed by the other half are no good. Not satisfied with that sort of sophistry, it follows through with two amazing sentences: "The terms and effects of the treaties between the Indian people and the government are widely misunderstood. A plain reading of the words used in the treaties reveals the limited and minimal promises which were included in them."

In this portion of the white paper the government lays bare its contempt for Indian treaties and indicates plainly that it does not recognize them as lawful obligations or even moral obligations. The white paper goes as far as to imply that Indians have completely misinterpreted the treaties and suggests that only the wise men of the government really understand what the treaties mean. This is not new. The government always has taken the position that its interpretation of the treaties was the only valid interpretation and, conversely, that such matters could not be understood by simple savages. The government thinks that a plain reading of the treaties shows them to be "limited and minimal."

The Indians think that, too. The position of the Indian people always has been that a plain reading of the treaties is inadequate and more than that, unjust. Simple, literal reading of the treaties does not reflect the spirit in which they were signed. The Indian long has realized and has said clearly that all the promises made to the Indian at the signing of the various treaties were never in fact written into the articles of the treaties. It is doubtful, however, that, had the promises not been made, any treaties would have been signed. The authors of the white paper, deliberately ignoring this historical fact, apparently without any concept of moral justice and without taking into consideration Indian pleas for an independent autonomous body to define the treaties, simply, with a wave of a pen, set out to destroy the treaties.

The authors go further. They claim: "The significance of the treaties in meeting the economic, educational, health and welfare needs of the Indian people has always been limited and will continue to decline." Quite the opposite. The position taken firmly by the Indians always has been that the treaties, if properly interpreted and implemented, would play a significant role in meeting such needs.

The crux of the situation remains that the government has never lived up to its obligations. Consequently, the needs of the Indians in all social and economic areas have never been properly met. For the authors of the white paper to claim that "the services that have been provided go far beyond what could have been foreseen by those who signed the treaties" is more than a gross distortion of fact. Simply stated, it is a deliberate, white-faced lie.

The white paper goes on to say: "The Government and the Indian people must reach a common understanding of the future role of the treaties." That statement borders on the ludicrous. There *never* can be a common understanding, unless the government radically redefines its position on the matter or agrees with the Indians to place their respective positions before an international tribunal qualified to give an unbiased judgment and settlement. The government, of course, dares not do this. They fear the almost certain result.

The policy proposal concludes its section on treaties by suggesting: "Finally, once Indian lands are securely within Indian control, the anomaly of treaties between groups within society and the government of that society will require that these treaties be reviewed to see how they can be equitably ended." What the government really is saying is that, by redefining the status of Indian lands and by legislating the Indian out of existence, they will terminate the treaties as they see fit. They will then unilaterally declare such termination equitable. This is how the government proposes to deal with the treaty Indian, half of Canada's Indian population. He is to earn his place in the Just Society by disappearing.

Yet the treaty Indians are lucky compared to the other half of the Indian population. For them the government has a casual brush-off in a mere four sentences. It says: "Other grievances have been asserted in more general terms. It is possible that some of these can be verified by appropriate research and may be susceptible of specific remedies. Others relate to aboriginal claims to land. These are so general and undefined that it is not realistic to think of them as specific claims capable of remedy except through a policy and program that will end injustice to Indians as members of the Canadian community." In effect, the government boasts that it does not recognize the legitimate aboriginal claims and other rights of the Indians of Quebec, British Columbia, the Yukon and much of the Northwest Territories. The government here is telling those Indians who have legitimate claims, arising from the fact that they never surrendered title to their land, that they cannot expect a just settlement. In twentieth-century Canada it is hard to believe that the government can embrace such a Machiavellian, barbaric concept of justice—yet there it is in the white paper. That is what the government proposes.

In the last portion of section five, the government proposes to appoint a commissioner who will inquire into and report upon how claims may be adjudicated. He will classify the claims that, in his judgment, ought to be referred to the courts or any special quasi-judicial body that may be recommended. He will also be authorized to recommend appropriate support to the new National Indian Brotherhood Committee on Indian

Rights and Treaties, so that it may conduct research on the behalf of Indians and so that it may assist the commissioner in his duties.

The Liberal government since 1965 has promised the Indians of Canada that it would set up an Indian claims commission. In the winter of 1968, the Honourable Mr. Chrétien assured Indian leaders that consultation was to take place on the terms of reference of the claims commission which he promised would be created during the 1969 session of Parliament. In June of 1969, the same man rose to state that he had "serious doubts as to whether a claims commission as proposed in 1965 is the right way to deal with the grievances of Indians put forward as claims."

The minister spent a lot of his time on the concept of equality in the opening sections of his policy statement, yet on the question of claims and the concept of treaty rights, he coolly denies the Indian the legal equality to place his claims before the courts of the country or before any special judicial body unless such claims have been sanctioned by the commissioner. The commissioner? Oh yes, the scrupulously fair commissioner, who will be appointed by the government, who will be responsible to the government which appointed him, whose only loyalties will be to the government. Whom does the minister think he is kidding? How can the Indian expect just treatment from a political appointee whose boss is the adversary in any confrontation? The only claims that the commissioner might be expected to submit for adjudication will be those of a token nature that will make the government look good but will not cost too much. Some will go through to allow the government to maintain its façade of equitable settlement to Indians for public scrutiny.

We are expected to stand still for the same sort of underhanded dealings with the work of our national committee. The national consultation meetings created a national committee to conduct independent research into the question of Indian rights and, upon settlement of that question, to participate in the drafting of a new Indian act. The white paper authors neatly devised the means by which the government could control and frustrate the work of that committee. In authorizing the commissioner to recommend appropriate support to our committee and by directing the committee to assist the commissioner in his enquiry, the white paper effectively destroys the autonomy of the committee. The commissioner can control the committee absolutely by withholding recommendations for financial assistance, thus ensuring that the committee not function because it lacks funds to do the job.

The government can move fast when it thinks it needs to protect its own interests. The federal government called for a consultation meeting early in 1969, supposedly to listen to Indian views. The representatives of the Indians of Canada met for one week in early May of 1969 and set up the machinery through which they proposed to conduct consultation supported by proper and badly needed documentation. In less than two months the government about-faced and effectively destroyed or circumvented the machinery so hopefully set up by the Indians. And it has the gall to ask us to put our faith in the Just Society. Once more the federal government has failed miserably to understand what the Indians of Canada were saying and has utterly shattered whatever faith and trust it had generated through its publicly stated desire for meaningful consultation. The government consistently has maintained the position that broken treaties and bad faith were products of a bygone age. But to the Indian, injustice from government sources simply represents the norm; broken promises from the government, bad faith from the government —those things were true of the past, to be sure, but what is devastating is that they continue today and give every evidence of continuing into the future.

The last section of the policy proposals deals with the vital and difficult question of land. The federal government, with a deft touch, combines three issues that pose agonizing questions for the Indian and almost ensures continuing controversies that will cause division among the Indians locally, provincially and nationally. The three issues are the concept of Indian land ownership, the question of taxation and the definition of the word *Indian*. To deal legally with these three issues, changes in the *Indian Act* are necessary. Just in proposing such changes, the government once again has gone directly against the wishes of the national Indian consultation meeting, which ended in agreement that no changes in the *Indian Act* should occur until the question of Indian rights had been settled.

Different cultures and different peoples have different views as to their relationship to their environment and, specifically, to land. The idea that a human being should say that this piece of land or water or sky belongs to him has traditionally been a concept foreign to the Indian. To the Indian, land, water, the sky and all things natural were created by the Great Spirit; therefore, only he could claim title to them. To the Indian, land was something he could never claim as his. For him, the land was provided by the Great Spirit for him to use—not own. However, for an increasing number of Indians, the old concept is changing to meet the white concept of ownership; consequently, the plans of the federal government will create many thorny problems.

To others there is yet a different viewpoint. Reserve lands are thought of in a different way than those already described, the traditional and the white man's way. When the Indians signed treaties with the crown, they gave up certain portions of land that they had used before. They view the reserve lands as lands that they kept not only for themselves but for the generations to follow them. To this group, the question of land ownership cannot be settled, because they do not feel they have the right to decide on the status of their reserves unless they are able to consult with generations yet to be born.

The question of land title is one that will be approached differently by the respective provinces and probably by respective reserves. The government states: "Between the present system and the full holding of title in fee simple lie a number of intermediate states. The first step is to change the system under which ministerial decision is required for all that is done with Indian land." This statement by the white paper comes extremely close to a land ownership question posed in *Choosing a Path*. In fact, it comes so close that, to the suspicious, it might appear that the government had answered the question it sent the Indians without bothering to listen to the replies they gave.

The most interesting sentence under the land section reads: "The Government believes that each band must make its own decision as to the way it wants to take control of its land and the manner in which it intends to manage it." While in principle the theory is sound, one has to take into consideration some practical implications dredged from experience. In the past there has always been a tendency for the government to try for an agreement with one reserve on issues that were controversial, then to celebrate that agreement as one that should be accepted on all reserves. We must be careful that decisions made on one reserve are not allowed to jeopardize the status of other reserves. The government will try to divide and conquer, concentrating all its wiles on one reserve, then, using those results, toppling reserve after reserve until there no longer are any reserves left.

Hiding it under the cloak of land ownership, the federal government proposes to introduce taxation onto the reserves. It realizes that the question of taxation will receive the most strenuous opposition from all the reserves but says it will take all the time needed for implementation.

"The Government believes that full ownership implies many things. It carries with it the free choice of use, of retention or of disposition. In our society it also carries with it an obligation to pay for certain services. The Government recognizes that it may not be acceptable to put all lands into the provincial systems immediately and make them subject to taxes. When the Indian people see that the only way they can own and fully control land is to accept taxation the way other Canadians do, they will make that decision."

Under the treaties, reserve lands were given a tax-free status, because the Indians felt that their surrender of land was full and more than sufficient compensation for the services the Canadian government was to provide in payment. In fact, to the Indian, the rights that he holds are continuing payments still owed by the government for the resources he gave up. Just the value of mineral resources contained within the land surrendered by the Indian would pay for all the services the government could provide for the next millennium. Certainly the four or five dollars a year that the government provides for the Indian would never even begin to pay for the value of land and resources taken by the government from the Indian. In effect, the Canadian government is asking the Indians of Canada to pay twice for services that they receive. The federal government is reneging on its commitments and, at the same time, trying to sell its immoral and illegal stand by drawing on the sacred cow of citizen responsibility.

One of the more perplexing problems faced by the Indian continues to be the question of band membership—the specific question of who should or should not belong to a reserve. After five or six decades during which the government has hopelessly fouled up the question legally, at the same time seriously dividing Indians, it now proposes to throw the whole mess it created into the laps of the Indians. This issue will create division more sharply than before and will serve to divert the energies of Indian people in wrong directions at a time when all their energy is required to move forward. The MacDonald-Chrétien doctrine proposes: "The qualifications for band membership which it has imposed are part of the legislation—the Indian Act—governing the administration of reserve lands. Under the present Act, the Government applies and interprets these qualifications. When bands take title to their lands, they will be able to define and apply these qualifications themselves."

Typically, the government states that it "is prepared to transfer to the Indian people the reserve lands, full control over them and, subject to the proposed Indian Lands Act, the right to determine who shares in ownership." The Indian Lands Act . . . well. We have yet to be told what will be contained in this new legislation, but from all indications it appears that the government plans a legislative device which will enable it to control the Indians without being held responsible for the consequences. It hopes to manage this by throwing the political problems into the laps of the respective provinces with nothing more hopeful in store for Indians in the way of genuine social change.

The MacDonald-Chrétien doctrine promises to take what little the Indian has, and offers in return increased frustration and disillusionment with the government. If the intention of the federal Indian policy was to ensure failure in meeting the problems the Indians face and to increase their sense of frustration and hostility toward the government of this country, then the Honourable Mr. Chrétien and his depute minister, John A. MacDonald, must be commended, for they have been brilliantly successful.

Ironically, the white paper concludes by talking about the implementation process, calling upon Indian organizations at both provincial and federal levels to assist. It states: "The Government proposes to ask that the associations act as the principal agencies through which consultation and negotiations would be conducted, but each band would be consulted about gaining ownership to its land holdings." It is difficult to envision any responsible Indian organization willing to participate in a proposal that promises to take the rights of all Indians away and attempts to define and legislate Indians out of existence. It is a strange government and a strange mentality that would have the gall to ask the Indian to help implement its plan to perpetrate cultural genocide on the Indians of Canada. It is like asking the doomed man on the gallows if he would mind pulling the lever that trips the trap.

Surely the government cannot seriously expect to receive any cooperation from the Indians of Canada in this proposal. For new discussions to take place, the government will have radically to change its conceptual framework to reflect the desires and wishes of the Indian. Until such time as it is willing to change, government pronouncements will continue to be received by the Indian as myths that bear no relationship to the realities of life.

As far as the white paper is concerned, the following phrase coined by an editor in the Northwest Territories neatly sums up the Indian feeling: "It is a white paper for white people created by the white elephant."

When the Curtain Comes Down

Cultural Renaissance or Civil Disorder?

The Indian has reached the end of an era. The things that we hold sacred, the things that we believe in have been repudiated by the federal government. But we will not be silenced again, left behind to be absorbed conveniently into the wretched fringes of a society that institutionalizes wretchedness. The Buckskin Curtain is coming down.

The Indian, and with him the larger Canadian society, faces two alternatives—a future in which the Indian may realize his potential through the provision of the essential resources which are rightfully his, or a future where frustrations are deepened by a continued state of deprivation leading to chaos and civil disorder.

Many factors, some of them still beyond his control, will influence the Indian's choice. His choice will not be an answer to the question of who he is; that can never change. Rather, his choice will lie in how he decides to protect and build his sense of identity; his choice hinges upon his definition of the role he will play in modern society.

I will outline the steps I feel are necessary before the Indian can begin to develop his full potential, the action needed to solve the many problems the Indians of Canada face.

Such action can come only through effective strengthening of existing Indian organizations. The first step is the provision of the resources needed to enable the National Indian Brotherhood to become an effective coordinating body, so that it may provide its member organizations with a national voice. The second step is the creation of strong and viable provincial organizations across the land.

Simultaneously, and coordinated with the strengthening of Indian organizations from national to local levels, the Indian must initiate action on four vital fronts: federal government recognition of all Indian rights must be secured; new concepts in education which can bridge the gap between our people and modern society must be found and introduced; restructured social institutions based on the community itself must be fashioned and broadly based economic development, sufficient to free the Indian at last from his subservient role, must be managed.

Within the next five years the Department of Indian Affairs is to be abolished. That is the one welcome aspect of the new government policy, but from a practical point of view, some interim body will have to be created. The duties and responsibilities of the department will be passed on to other federal agencies, and from past Indian experience, we know that all government departments have a tendency to pass the buck from one to another. To meet this prospect, the National Indian Brotherhood can play the role of a human resources authority, coordinating the services offered to the Indian by the many federal departments. This role would save the Indian many headaches and aid him in all his dealings with the federal government. At the same time the brotherhood would be in a position to help the various government agencies establish priorities in relation to the needs of the Indians of Canada.

Because of its political structure, the Indian people are assured of continuing control over the activities of the National Indian Brotherhood. This enables the Indians of Canada to participate in the democratic process and assures them an active role in the broad workings of government. In practical terms, this may be the closest the Indians of Canada can come to achieving Prime Minister Trudeau's concept of participatory democracy.

The tough, pragmatic problem solving must take place at the provincial and local levels, and this is the reason provincial Indian organizations must be made as strong as possible. The nature of these primary organizations necessarily must be political. Auxiliary organizations also can be created to work in close harness with the political bodies, to carry the task of concentrating Indian efforts on economic problems and solutions. Such auxiliary organizations can serve effectively in the fields of research and development, but the major provincial organizations must be political, because only through political vehicles can the Indian people express their needs and create pressure for their programmes.

One new role that Indian organizations must play lies in the area of restoring and revitalizing a sense of direction, a sense of purpose and a sense of being. The white man in the last century has effectively killed the sense of worth in the Indian. Many factors, some of which I have dealt with in earlier chapters, have been responsible for the psychological and spiritual crisis of the Indian. The political organization must be the core of an effort to redefine the word *Indian* in such a way that our people can begin to develop a positive sense of identity.

Perhaps over the long term the most important responsibility the local organization must assume is the creation of a new order of leadership. This must be a leadership that will know and be able to relate positively to the traditions of the past, to the culture of our people and at the same time be tuned into life in the twentieth and twenty-first centuries. Above all, this must be a leadership totally committed to the Indian peoples. It must be a leadership that cannot be corrupted or bought off by those who would support the status quo so that they may continue their stagnating and stifling hold on our people.

The Indian must see his provincial organization in a new perspective. There must be a consolidation of all the scattered, ineffective local organizations into strong provincial, political bodies. In order for this to happen, present leaders must reassess seriously their positions and their motives in occupying them. They must learn to put the interest of their people above their own personal needs and desires. This is happening, but the process has not yet been completed. Consequently, forces of the federal government in too many instances still are able to divide our people by skillful catering to the psychological needs of some of them. Until all our leaders have learned to subordinate personal ambition to their peoples' wishes, the Indians of Canada will remain weak and divided.

The new generation of Indians looks to its leaders for guidance, for example and for a sense of purpose. No more vital responsibility for the new leadership of our provincial organizations can be imagined.

For the scattered and isolated reserves which can be found in every province, the Indian organizations must work to create a sense of brotherhood to help weld these communities together into dynamic, growing forces that can participate in their twentieth-century environment. In the process of creating a new leadership, the provincial organizations must help these divided, forgotten communities find a common identity.

The Indian people of Canada must assume new confidence. There must be a rebirth of the Indian, free, proud, his own man, the equal of his fellow Canadian. Some naïvely believe that true equality will come to the Indian by dispensation from some outside force. It is not within the power of any outside force, be it the prime minister or any minister of the crown, to command equality. In twentieth-century Canada, equality comes only from economic strength, political power, good organization and through the pride and confidence of a people.

As long as the Indian does not have a positive image of himself, no Canadian, no human being will have a positive image of him and no one will ever respect him. There can be no equality as long as the dignity of the Indian is not respected. Today, most Canadians are either indifferent to Indians or hate them or pity them. The worst of the three is the man who pities the Indian, for he denies the object of his pity the opportunity to be a man. Canadian society will stop pitying the Indian and respect him only when the Indian has gained economic, political or organizational strength. A man who believes Canadian society will grant equality to the Indian because of its sense of Christian responsibility or its adherence to Christian beliefs or because of its obeisance to any concept of human rights common to all men, believes in myths. The Canadian society, self-righteously proclaiming itself just and civilized, has not extended equality to the Indian over the past century, and there is no reason to believe, expect or hope that it will change its spots over the next century if the Indian stays weak.

As the Indians of Canada are working to strengthen their organizations, they must initiate forward movement on other levels.

The Indian must have from the federal government immediate recognition of all Indian rights for the reestablishment, review and renewal of all existing Indian treaties. The negotiations for this must be undertaken in a new and different spirit by both sides. The treaties must be maintained. The treaties must be reinterpreted in light of needs that exist today. Such interpretation and application of the treaties by the Canadian government will help bring all generations of Indians together with a common sense of positive purpose. This is not a concept that should be strange to the government. The treaties differ little from the way the government deals with corporations or corporate bodies, and for that matter all segments of Canadian society, except Indians and possibly the poor of Canada.

Apparently, the government has been unable or unwilling to understand the importance of this concept to the Indians. The treaties, or the concept of Indian rights, must be respected, for they form a major factor in the question of Indian identity. The Indian simply cannot afford to allow the government to renege on its obligations because, if he does, he commits cultural suicide. This is the reason for the position adopted by the Indian people … that their rights are not and cannot be negotiable.

Almost equally important is the area of education. Here, too, both sides must move forward into new concepts. The institution of education is largely a cultural phenomenon. Since the introduction of formal white education to the Indians of Canada, their own original educational processes have either been shunted completely aside or discouraged. The only purpose in educating the Indian has been to create little brown white men, not what it should have been, to help develop the human being or to equip him for life in a new environment.

A new look must be given, then, to the fundamental purpose of educating the Indian. It is not enough for the government to promise it will change the content of history books more truly to tell the Indian story. In comparison to the real purpose of education, this is an almost frivolous approach. Of course we would like the falsehoods deleted and Indians characterized more truthfully in what the youth of Canada is taught, but Indians are much more interested in and must approach education with completely new ideas. Indian leaders must be given the opportunity to see and study the educational processes of different peoples in different countries. Only in this way can they help to develop a new conceptual framework related to education and to the solving of their own social problems.

I believe that different forms of education are both possible and available. The majority of our people do not have the opportunity to benefit from existing provincial institutions of education, especially those at the postsecondary level. Few of our people have sufficient academic background to make proper use of the technological schools, trade schools, colleges or universities. Even if they did, there would still be a need for some new form of education or institution that would help them develop a living, dynamic culture. For education to mean anything to our people a new kind of institution or process to bridge the gap between where we stand now and the available postsecondary institutions must be created. This means some form of temporary but special mass educational process. Indian initiative, channelled through our own organizations, must develop such institutions to enable our people to benefit from programmes now offered by existing educational systems.

These new institutions must be prepared to help Indians develop their sense of identity. The function of such institutions will lie in the areas of social rebuilding, psychological renewal and cultural renaissance. Indian organizations must operate these schools, for only they qualify for the task of identifying teachers and administrators with the resources to meet the cultural needs of Indians.

The white person must come to realize that the Indian cannot be a good Canadian unless he is first a responsible and a good Indian. Few Indians can discover a sense of purpose and direction from the white society. They must find such a sense of identity within themselves as human beings and as Indians before they can begin to work creatively with others. The government must understand this, because it is in this area that Canadian society can form a successful partnership with the Indian, in working together to find ways and means through which the educational process will develop human beings with purpose and direction.

The Indian communities themselves carry the responsibility for solving the social problems faced by Indians. Social development is irrevocably intertwined with leadership development, educational progress and economic advance. To tackle these problems the Indian communities will need extensive resources, both human and economic. The federal government's proposal to transfer all services to provincial governments does not solve anything. This changes nothing; it leaves the Indian in the same bogged-down bureaucratic predicament. Attempts to solve his social problems will still be initiated by people from the outside who know little and understand less of the Indian. It is true that the provincial governments can play a useful role in providing support services to Indian communities, but first there must be created, within the communities, structures that attack the problems at their source. Ideally, most of the services within a community should be provided by the community itself. Before this can happen, huge sums of money must be provided, aimed at community problems. No outside bureaucracy, whether in Ottawa or in a provincial capital, is flexible enough either to meet the problems head-on, or better yet, attack the causes. Before the local communities can take over such responsibility, skilled, highly trained leadership at the local level must be found. Once again, that premises educational institutions geared to the needs of the Indian and controlled by the Indian.

Service and support structures in the social field—recreation, welfare, special education programmes, community development and law and order—must be set up in every community. Creation of a provincial Indian police force, trained and equipped to handle problems in any community, should be supervised by provincial organizations. It seems reasonable to think that once an environment of self-reliance and independence exists, activities in which non-Indians can participate will develop naturally. From that foundation could grow cooperative ventures, both social and economic, which could help bring the races together, eliminating or dissipating to a large degree much existing bigotry. Racial cooperation is a two-way street. So far only the Indian has been expected to come the extra mile.

The Indian peoples of Canada are just beginning to be aware of the broad implications of economic development. Any progress to be made must be bolstered by basic sound economic programmes. For the first time the Indian peoples are beginning to realize that this means more than isolated, make-do farming, fishing, trapping or lumbering. Huge sums of money are needed to enable Indian groups to take advantage of economic development opportunities on our own reserves.

An economic development corporation, funded by both national and provincial levels of government, should be founded in each province. Qualified Indians must have control of such fund resources to enable them to finance the necessary programmes at the community level. Such development corporation funds would initiate research into the economic potential of every reserve, then get the necessary development programmes underway.

To handle properly matters like these, Indians must have the resources to hire the best brains in the country as consultants. Voluntary workers are not trained for such work. Indians will gain from the psychological advantage of knowing that such hired consultants are their employees, that they do not come as civil servants who in the process enslave the Indian. The Indian Association of Alberta, in preparing its policy paper in answer to the federal government's white paper, will go into detail in this area. For the purpose of this book it is sufficient to say that the subservient role of the Indian is fast drawing to a close.

I have dealt briefly with four areas in which I believe, given the opportunity, the Indian can more than fulfill his responsibilities to our country. There exists a belief among our people that we were given this country to share with all peoples and to ensure that its natural resources are used for the good of mankind. There exists also among the older generation of our people the feeling that the ancestors of the white people who came to our country came as human beings who were able to accept the Indians as human beings. Our elders believe that the process of time and a changing world has caused the descendants of those first white people to grow less sensitive toward the Indian and, for that matter, less sensitive toward any human being. Our older people think that it is part of the responsibility of the Indian to help the white man regain this lost sense of humanity. I believe that the Indian people are not afraid of responsibility; in fact, they welcome the chance to play a new role in contemporary times. This can happen only if the rights of the Indian people are honoured, their dignity respected.

I have outlined some of what must happen if the Indian is to realize his potential and take part in today's world. We have seen what frustration, deprivation and misery can lead to in the United States and throughout the world. The young generation that is even now flexing its muscles does not have the patience that older leaders have shown. If the present leadership is unable to come to terms with the non-Indian society, unable to win respect for Indian rights and dignity, then the younger generation will have no reason to believe that the existing democratic political system has much meaning for them. They will not believe that the present system can work to change our situation. They will organize and organize well. But, driven by frustration and hostility, they will organize not to create a better society but to destroy your society, which they feel is destroying our people. This is the choice before the Indian; this is the fork in the road that the government and non-Indian society must recognize.

Controlling our choice of a path—the realization of the full potential of the Indian people, or despair, hostility and destruction—is our belief that the Indian must be an Indian. He cannot realize his potential as a brown white man. Only by being an Indian, by being simply what he is, can he ever be at peace with himself or open to others.

The present course of the federal government drives the Indian daily closer and closer to the second alternative ... despair, hostility, destruction.

References

Canada, Department of Citizenship and Immigration, Indian Affairs Branch. *The Administration of Indian Affairs*. Ottawa, 1964.
——. *New Directions in Indian Affairs*. Ottawa, 1964. (Notes for an address by René Tremblay to the Indian-Eskimo Association of Canada, in London, Ontario.)
——. *Observations on the Integration Program of the Education Division*. Ottawa, 1963.
Canada, Department of Indian Affairs and Northern Development. *Indian Policy: politique indienne*. Ottawa, 1969.
——. *Indians and the Law*. Ottawa, 1967. (A survey prepared for the Honourable Arthur Laing by the Canadian Corrections Association and the Canada Welfare Council.)
Hawthorn, Harry B., Marc-Adelard Tremblay et al. *A Survey of the Contemporary Indians of Canada*. Part I. Ottawa, 1967.
Wax, Rosalie H. and Robert K. Thomas. "American Indians and White People." *Phylon: The Atlanta University Review of Race and Culture*, Winter 1961.

Copies of the *Indian Act* (1951, c. 29, s. 1) and of the treaties concluded between the crown and Canadian Indians, with the respective adhesions and reports, are available from the Queen's Printer, Ottawa.

The reports of the *Indian Act* consultation meetings in Edmonton (12–13 December 1968) and Winnipeg (18–20 December 1968) are available from the Department of Indian Affairs and Northern Development.